CONCILIUM

Religion in the Eighties

CONCILIUM

General Secretariat: Prins Bernhardstraat 2, 6521 AB Nijmegen, The Netherlands

Concilium 197 (3/1988): Ecclesiastical Institutions

CONCILIUM

List of Members

Advisory Committee: Ecclesiastical Institutions

POWER
IN THE
CHURCH

Edited by
James Provost
and
Knut Walf

English Language Editor
James Aitken Gardiner

T. & T. CLARK LTD
Edinburgh

April 1988
ISBN: 0 567 30077 3

ISSN: 0010-5236

Typeset by C. R. Barber & Partners (Highlands) Ltd, Fort William
Printed by Page Brothers (Norwich) Ltd

Concilium: Published February, April, June, August, October, December.
Subscriptions 1988: UK: £27.50 (including postage and packing); USA: US$49.95 (including air mail postage and packing); Canada: Canadian$59.95 (including air mail postage and packing); other countries: £27.50 (including postage and packing).

CONTENTS

Concilium 197 Special Column

Terrorism. An Irish Perspective
SEAN FREYNE   xi

POWER IN THE CHURCH

Editorial: Power in the Church
JAMES PROVOST
KNUT WALF   xvii

Part I

The Concept of Power in the Church: New Testament
Perspectives
JOSEF BLANK   3

Power in the Church: an Historico–critical Survey
JOHN LYNCH   13

Sex and Power in the Church
ERIC FUCHS   23

Power in the Contemporary Church: Sociological Theories
KARL GABRIEL   29

The Exercise of Power in Today's Church
WIGAND SIEBEL   39

Part II

The Competence of Priests, Prophets and Kings
HERVI RIKHOF   53

Auctoritas – potestas – jurisdictio – facultas – officium –
munus: a conceptual analysis
RIK TORFS   63

Proper and Vicarious Power in the Church
  AUGUSTINE MENDONCA   74

Legitimation and Bureaucratisation of Ecclesial Power
  PATRICK GRANFIELD   86

The Exercise of Power and the Principle of Submission
  PATRICK VALDRINI   94

Part III

The Power of the Church and the Powers of Evil
  JOSEPH COMBLIN   105

Attitudes of Heart and Mind
  SHARON HOLLAND   110

Those with no Mandate in the Church
  PIERO ANTONIO BONNET   115

Power in the Church of England
  STEPHEN SYKES   123

Contributors   129

CONCILIUM 197 Special Column

Sean Freyne

Terrorism. An Irish Perspective

ACT OF terror upon act of terror; violent death following violent death; funeral after deadly funeral—a self-perpetuating cycle of human destruction. This is the seemingly endless plot of the drama that re-enacts itself daily in the streets of Northern Ireland. Our newspapers can occasionally spare a few inches for coverage of atrocities elsewhere— Beirut, South Africa, Nicaragua, Sri Lanka—telling of stories that are so different, and yet so similar to ours. Different scripts, other actors, and yet the same sad, senseless ending.

It is so easy to be engulfed in the midst of it all, torn emotionally between this side and that. Stories of para-military atrocities and of mindless state violence compete with each other for a hearing, told by those who—on both sides—have little interest in objectivity. And then there are the condemnations: the ritual condemnations of each killing by churchmen and politicians, neither capable of changing the scenario, it would seem, yet obliged to be 'outraged' and sadly searching for the fresh pejorative that will strike the correct note for ears dulled by trite repetition.

The theologian cannot remain a detached commentator on such events. Conflicting feelings well up—anger, hatred, disgust, frustration, pity, faltering love, forgiveness ... Yet in the midst of so much human misery some sense of distance is called for if one wishes to make helpful comment; not the distance of detachment, but the distance that can allow some ray of gospel hope to emerge by suggesting how it might be possible to transform communal hatred into a praxis of human togetherness and tolerance of cultural and religious pluralism.

If the spoken or written word is to release new energy into a situation deadened by platitudes, precision of thought and expression is called for. Unfortunately, 'terrorism' and 'terrorist' must now feature high on the list of such platitudes. Far from achieving the aim of those who employ them to vilify those engaged in acts of violence against the state, they have become—in other circles—glorious labels. Such relatively moderate terms as 'patriot' and 'patriotism', or even the traditionally more glamorous 'freedom-fighters', have been pushed to one side. This trend in our language patterns should tell us much about the direction in which we are headed.

The terminology of terrorism can be of little assistance in analysing the motives that generate acts of violence against the state and its defenders, or in unmasking the assumptions of those who seek to deal with their perpetrators by strong-arm tactics in the name of law and order. The real terrorist, so the counter-rhetoric claims, is the state with its under-cover agents, its biased judicial system and its own forms of violent activity.

With a few notable exceptions, political analysts tend to ignore the historic roots of the current problems. The assumption of present-day administrators is that once offending legislation has been changed and other forms of social injustice removed all should now be forgiven and forgotten by those who have experienced alienation and oppression for so long. But folk memory does not function in that way. Past oppressions enter the living culture through song, story and other forms of ritual re-enactment and remain deeply embedded. In such a climate each act of the authorities is filtered through a negative hermeneutic of suspicion. Active awareness of this must surely be the first step for those seeking to de-legitimise the so-called 'terrorists' as defenders of the rights of the minority. The past should neither be defended nor ignored because it is indefensible. A fresh recognition of this would be much more productive symbolically in terms of law and order than all the reiteration of the state's determination to wipe out terrorism. That battle has been lost. It is now a question of who can best make the symbol system work to the advantage of their vision.

Those who seek to destabilise or destroy the state and its machinery through violent acts have a much better sense of the power of symbolic action. The funeral of the hero or heroine who has died 'in action' has traditionally been used for the defiant proclamation of the 'gospel'. The security forces have never been able to deal with such events and invariably have fallen into the trap of being, or being cast in the role of disrupters of a sacred occasion. In the week that these words are penned five people have already met with violent deaths in the course of funerals. 'Let the dead bury their dead' has a sinister ring in such a setting, a far cry from the life-centred concerns of the one who uttered that shocking word.

The 'movement', as it is euphemistically called by its supporters, betrays other aspects of a religious phenomenon. Its leaders claim to be the sole guardians and only authentic interpreters of the national myths and symbols. A strict internal code of discipline is maintained, resulting in the punishment of offenders by knee-capping or killing, if the crime is deemed sufficiently grave. An ascetic, even puritanical image is cultivated as part of the legitimisation process. Issues of social justice for the oppressed are championed at local level at the price of support for the armed-resistance struggle.

It adds considerably to the intractable nature of the current situation that both sides can appeal to various elements of the Judeo-Christian story in support of their claims. 'The movement' finds in Easter a highly appropriate set of images, particularly the power of blood sacrifice and the Rising itself, while the extreme Protestants find in the Biblical images of Exodus and land a fruitful source for their own foundation and legitimisation myths.

Where in this context, can the gospel of Jesus of Nazareth begin to function critically while pointing the way forward? Repeated condemnation of each terrorist action by Church leaders is scarcely adequate, while refusing at the same time to take the bold step out of the ghettoes of cultural Catholicism and cultural Protestantism. The situation is too pressing to wait for 'official' ecumenists to set the agenda, while the sectarian myth-makers hijack the Christian story in the name of violence. A radical experiment in Christian living is called for, since it is—quite literally—a matter of life and death. Small communities where the beatitudes of peace-making and hungering and thirsting for justice are being fostered on an inter-denominational basis need the active support and encouragement of the Churches, if the lonely middle ground between the opposing extremes of violence and counter-violence is to be peopled with real signs of the kingdom of justice and peace. It is a challenge that the Irish churches seem all too reluctant to take on—in education, in worship and in living a common witness. Yet, from a Christian perspective it seems to embody the best hope of an answer to our problems.

Note that this Special Column, like others in this series, is written under the sole responsibility of the author.

POWER IN THE CHURCH

Editorial
Power in the Church

WHEN ONE speaks of 'power' in connection with 'Church', this awakens many thought associations—and also, of course, emotions. That 'Church' has something to do with 'power' will not be denied even by those who reject such a connection in principle, or who try to legitimise the facts purely theologically by drawing attention to the exceptional nature of the Church in comparison with other social groups. The Church is a social system like (say) families, societies, parties or states which possess 'as a rule an accumulation of power' (Wigand Siebel). As law, consequently also canon law, represents a factor in the emergence and maintenance of power, so it is reasonable for experts in canon law and representatives from related disciplines constantly to reflect the phenomenon of power in the Church, in their capacities both as those affected and as those responsible.

Although there is no precise mention of concrete examples of the exercise of power in the Church in this edition of CONCILIUM, every reflection of this theme has concrete dimensions. As soon as one approaches the basis of the subject, that is the legitimisation of power, one meets very concrete difficulties. Is there a legitimisation of power (in the Church) valid at all times, or are power (and authority) in the Church subject to changes, conditioned by the prevailing historical-cultural context? And how can one imagine an answer to that question in view of differing but simultaneous contexts?

In the tradition of the Roman Church one spoke officially up to the present day (although never without being challenged by one's own misgivings and by criticism within the church) of 'sacra potestas', the sacred power or authority of the Church's leaders ('spiritual shepherds') standing in the succession of the Apostles. The first Book of Law of the Roman Church, the Codex Iuris Canonici of 1917 also used the word 'potestas' in an almost inflationary way. The majority of the fathers of the Second Vatican Council wanted not only to curb the use of this concept, but even to replace it by another which seemed to them more suited to expressing the particular characteristic of ecclesiastical power and authority. It was decided, falling back on a term from reforming ecclesiology, to use the word *munus* which can only be translated into modern language in an analogous way: task, service but also office. 'Munus' is therefore a polysemantic, analogous concept—like 'power' itself (Josef Blank points this out). It is therefore also no surprise that, in the conception of the new Codex Iuris Canonici which was to transpose the doctrines of the Second Vatican Council into the rules of the Church, difficulties arose in the use of the concept 'munus'. That the authors of the new codex all too easily then made frequent use of the traditional concept 'potestas' may be understandable, but is—on theological grounds—incomprehensible. The richness of traditional legal language could also have put at their disposal a good many concepts which, in not a few instances, would have been better suited and also more accurate then 'potestas': 'facultas' for example, or even auctoritas. And where, in the new codex, one speaks occasionally of 'munus', it would have been better to use the concept 'officium' (Rik Torfs).

Terminological vagueness is however only a symptom that much of the content is also in disarray. Power and its legitimisation are, in our opinion, far too seldom turned into matters for debate in the Church. On a given occasion one will, if need be, discuss the exercise of power (Patrick Granfield), particularly if it is not without dispute in relation to concrete examples (think of Church disciplinary proceedings on teaching against people like Boff, Curran, Küng, Pfürtner,[1] Pohier or Schillebeeckx).

Many and indeed also profound inadequacies in the exercise of power by ecclesiastical authorities are consequences of the 'sacred bureaucracy' which is how our Church appears today in not a few particular Churches, although in the case of the institution of the Roman Curia this has been so for some time now. Although it was in the early twenties that Max Weber gave a hitherto unsurpassed and accurate description of the centralisation of power and its bureaucratisation (Karl Gabriel), his references, critical in their intent, have been almost without consequence for the further exercise of ecclesiastical power structures. Centralisation and, with it, bureaucratisation have been continued and carried through at all levels of the Church, whatever the reasons might be. This, it is true, applies principally to the running of the Church and to the structures of those particular Churches which, because of their membership numbers and finances, are particularly strong. But this also has consequences for the 'weaker' and hence dependent particular Churches (especially in the so-called Third World) which, for reasons of financial support, have to deal with those bureaucracies and their power.

That 'power in the Church' or 'power of the Church' does not however always have to have a negative implication can be seen in examples from the 'Third World'. In Latin America in particular, Christians have re-discovered the 'power' of their bishops in the struggle against oppression and structural, that is politically created, poverty (Joseph Comblin). But it is just this complex social context which makes clear that it is here not a question of power in the usual sense of the word but rather the 'authority' of the bishops and of their office which gives them power over the powerful and at the same time often makes them the last refuge of the powerless.

This 'power' is not one's own, it is rather a vicarious power, conferred by the Lord of the Church. We are aware of the ambivalence of this statement. History has given sufficient proof of that. Properly understood, this conception of power in the Church is a protection against the abuse of power and arrogance. And understood in this way, power 'potestas' is service (*munus*). But '... en catholicisme, le pouvoir s'avance toujours sous le masque du sacré, c'est-à-dire peu ou prou de l'interdit' (H. Chaigne, quoted by Eric Fuchs).[2] The religious grounds for 'power in the Church' constitute probably its greatest danger. They relieve it of any (further) legitimisation, make it unchallengeable and raise it above the passage of the times. So a critical analysis of a very concrete and often painfully felt exercise of power is penalised by an interdict, that is by a ban which is connected with a threat of punishment. Those who question, who follow their conscience, experience this power in the Church up to the present day: those, for example, who question the handed-town teaching of the Church; or women who are not satisfied with the role allotted them with reference to traditions; and unfortunately in many parts of the Church still also the poor, those without possessions or political rights. The 'power of the Church' was and often is remote for those who need it most. We remember here the silence of the Church in Nazi Germany when millions of Jewish fellow-citizens were sent to their deaths. We remember also the weakness of a powerful Church in Argentina when the junta was in power.

A theological reflection—and indeed also a canonical one—of the theme 'power in the Church' undoubtedly reaches into political realms. We know that the powerful in the Church react much more quickly to such considerations and discussions than to any that touch on central theological doctrine. This must make us attentive; and at the same time it makes clear the importance of this theme and its discussion. It is of course not possible in this issue to describe and reflect this theme comprehensively in all its aspects. But it is the wish of the authors in this issue to stimulate further thoughts. For that we thank them.

James Provost
Knut Walf

Translated by Gordon Wood

Notes

1. See for example Ludwig Kaufmann *Ein ungelöster Kirchenkonflikt: Der Fall Pfürtner* (Fribourg 1987).
2. '... in Catholicism power always advances behind the facade of the sacred, that is to say more or less, of the interdict'.

PART I

Josef Blank

The Concept of 'Power' in the Church: New Testament Perspectives

1. GENERAL INTRODUCTORY REMARKS ON THE CONCEPT OF 'POWER'

THE CONCEPT of 'power'[1] belongs to those polysemantic, analogous concepts which cannot be defined in an abstract way; they must always be viewed in their concrete frame of reference, in their theological, legal, political or social context. According to classical tradition one should distinguish between *potestas* and *auctoritas*, between 'power' as an area of competence and authority, above all in the realm of the state, and 'power' as non-violent, predominantly spiritual and rationally justified authority or aura,[2] as in the famous letter from Pope Gelasius I to Emperor Anastasius in the year 494: *Duo quippe sunt, imperator auguste, quibus principaliter mundus hic regitur: auctoritas sacrata pontificum et regalis potestas* ('There are two things, illustrious emperor, by which this world is primarily ruled: the sacred authority of the bishops and imperial power').[3] 'Power' is also a fundamental religious term, above all as 'numinous power': 'Power has a peculiar quality which strikes human beings as dangerous; that which is dangerous is not however holy, but that which is holy is dangerous ... Power awakens in the human soul a feeling of timidity which expresses itself as fear and attraction.'[4] One may assume that all power, even in the secularised state, touches deep down on religion and its problems in a way that can only be hinted at here. Belief in God automatically confers the title 'all-powerful', *omnipotens*, on God. God 'has' no power which could be taken back from Him, instead He is omnipotence, He is *potens per se ipsum*. Also, in the idea of God, abundance of power coincides with an abundance of all that is good and meaningful, so that 'injustice' is fundamentally excluded. At this point however a typical problem arises which was only intensified by belief in Christ: God's omnipotence as a unity of power and meaning is not experienced and perceived as such in the world and history, but rather as the impotence and absence of God; injustice, meaninglessness and evil exercise direct rule. World, society, military power etc. appear to us as much more powerful than God and Jesus Christ. The Epistle to the Hebrews already comments on this: 'For it was not to angels that God subjected the world to come, of which we are speaking (but rather to the Son) ... Now in putting everything in subjection to him, he left nothing outside his control. As it is, we do not yet see everything in subjection to him (Hebrews 2:5.8). God's power appears as powerlessness; in powerlessness and weakness God's power can be at its strongest (cf. 2 Cor. 12:9). Here the concept of power becomes dialectical and paradoxical, the *theologia crucis*. In actual fact 'power', as well as 'authority', 'the authority of office' etc. are, in theology, never to be understood 'unambiguously', as a mere legitimising formula, as a 'supreme principle' from which 'auctoritas' or 'potestas' could be directly derived; it is rather a question of a 'dialectical concept': no office and no authority, no service performed in the community stands outwith the Cross of Christ. A particular characteristic of ecclesiastical power is an especial form of 'powerlessness': ecclesiastical directives, for example, can, it is true, lay claim to 'authority', but they are, unlike those within the state, absolutely unenforceable, except by financial pressure or by express withdrawal of authority, that is to say, only within the hierarchy of office.

2. THE GENERALLY ACCEPTED CHRISTOLOGICAL—SOTERIOLOGICAL MEANING OF 'POWER'

All power and authority in the *Ecclesia Dei et Jesu Christi* is fundamentally the power and authority of Christ and should be understood and derived from this 'christological principle of power'. First and foremost the words of the risen Christ are valid here: 'All authority (*exousia, potestas*) in heaven and on earth has been given to me. Go therefore and make disciples of all nations, baptising them in the name of the Father and of the Son and of the Holy Spirit, teaching them to observe all that I have commanded you; and lo, I am with you always, to the close of the age' (Matt. 28:18–20). Even if in these words of the risen Christ it is not a question of an authentic word of Jesus but of a 'fashioning of the Evangelist and his community',[5] we can still see here how the Evangelist Matthew views and judges spiritual authority in the Christian

Church, that is as 'the authority of Jesus Christ'. That he understands this exclusively and in a unique way, can be seen for instance in the statements in Matt. 23:8–12: 'For you have one Master ... and you are all brethren ...' All power in heaven and earth is given to the 'Christ raised on high'; He participates directly in the power and sovereignty of God. Arising from these explanations we see 'the Lordship of Jesus Christ and the reality of the Church as carrying the main emphasis. Both realities are closely related to one another and are often mutually explanatory: we find on the one hand the Church's confession of the authority of the kyrios and of His omnipresence, and on the other hand the concept of the disciple portrayed there and the command to proselytise'.[6] This is no special theology on the part of Matthew, but this is said in a more or less similar fashion in the Hymn to Christ in the Epistle to the Philippians (Phil. 2:6–11):[7] in the resurrection or most closely linked to it, God has raised Jesus beyond all measure and conferred on Him the 'name which is above every other name'; the expression meant is '*kyrios*/lord', so that the whole universe must confess: '*Kyrios Jesous Christos* to the glory of God the Father'. We do not need to deal with the religio-historical problems of this text in any more detail here; only to say in passing that the question of 'hellenistic' origin or of adopting ideas from the mystery cults does not arise. Here rather we have the theme of the 'raising of Christ to the right hand of God' in the sense of Psalm 110,[8] of the enthronement of Jesus Christ as the heavenly *pantocrator* (see Rev. 1:12–20, and chapters 4–5). The decisive factor here is that the 'Christ raised on high' as absolute bearer of authority and Lord over the Church *and* over the world and history is always seen in His lasting identity as the crucified Jesus of Nazareth. Church and Christian belief recognise this divine and all-embracing sovereignty of the Christ raised on high. This is also expressed in the briefest wording of the confession of faith: *Kyrios Jesous*/Jesus is Lord; 'Therefore I want you to understand that no one speaking by the Spirit of God ever says "Jesus be cursed!" and no one can say "Jesus is Lord" except by the Holy Spirit' (1 Cor. 12:3). Or: 'If you confess with your lips that Jesus is Lord and believe in your heart that God raised him from the dead, you will be saved. For man believes with his heart and so is justified, and he confesses with his lips and so is saved' (Rom. 10:9–10). The confession of the kyrios Jesus Christ and His sovereignty is, according to Paul, the *specificum Christianum* which by its nature founds a Church and makes a precise distinction between this Church and both Judaism and all heathen religions as well as the mystery cults. It is also the personal confession of all Christians, regardless of which level they occupy and which offices or charisms they possess; in this respect, there is not the slightest difference between ordinary Christians and office bearers. Conversely there can be no release for Christians from this sphere of sovereignty and power; nor can they wish for that in any way; for it is just this power and sovereignty of Jesus Christ over believers which in the first instance really guarantees them 'justice and salvation', resurrection and eternal life. There cannot therefore be, in a concrete sense, a 'Church free of sovereignty';[9] because man outside of the Church—at least as Paul sees it—would, lacking security or standards, be exposed to idols, demons and all the powers of evil. As man is basically a conditioned being, a certain relative 'freedom from sovereignty' is indeed possible, but in no way can it be complete or absolute. Either man stands under the sovereignty of God and Christ for his salvation, or he stands under the sovereignty of the gods and strange powers; the theme is by no means an uncommon one. Release from the sovereignty of Christ is therefore only an apparent freedom, whereas only submission to the sovereignty of Christ in the obedience of belief guarantees the true liberation and freedom of man.

A further important feature of the 'sovereignty of Jesus Christ' is its 'ever-present nature'.[10] The Church which stands as a whole under the sovereignty of Christ—and it is just this fact that the Church is the area or sphere in which this sovereignty counts for something, in which it possesses unquestionable validity and no longer needs to show especial 'authorisation', which is a part of the 'essential being of the Church'—this Church does not deal solely or primarily with the purely 'historical Jesus' but with the ever-present Lord Jesus Christ. A simply profane and unbelieving view of things does of course see it differently;[11] all that it can see is purely history, the simple past. What is important for the New Testament is every new presence of Jesus in the life of His community; this is a totally different point of view. Hence the validity of the promise '... and, lo, I am with you always, to the close of the age' (Matt. 28:20b). What is at stake here is the ever-present help of the *kyrios*. Matt.28:20 is, as it were, the 'Christianisation' of the Old Testament-Judaic commitment by JHWH to help His people. 'What always matters is active help, JHWH's presence in the events of history, not His presence in a static ritual, tied to one particular locality.'[12] At all events, one must give greater consideration, with regard to the post-exilic period, to the 'ritual presence' of JHWH, above all in the Temple; with the destruction of the second Temple in 70 AD, the Jewish community was faced with a renewed consideration of the question of God's presence, his *schekkina*. For 'Judaism' this 'presence of God' is mainly connected with the Torah and the study of the Torah: if two, or according to another version ten people, are gathered together and devote themselves to the study of the Torah, then *schekkina* is amongst them.[13] For Christians on the other hand, Jesus Christ is the 'place of God's presence', as is quite strongly emphasised in John's Gospel.[14] All this means: in all that it is and does the Church is continually referred back to Jesus Christ, the earthly Jesus, crucified and risen. In this sense it has no 'independent' existence; time and again it must take its bearings from Jesus Christ, above all as He speaks to us in the New Testament. The power of God and Christ cannot and should not be understood according to 'profane' (sociological or legal) ideas of power (as 'projections' of social or economic ideas and conditions). For both the power of JHWH and of Jesus Christ have a basically *soteriological structure*; 'power' has here a positive goal, a creative content: that is the redemption and liberation of man, his life. JHWH brings about salvation for His people; the very fact that Jesus did not cling on to 'power', 'as if it were plunder', brought about the true redemption of man. The commandments too (e.g. the Ten Commandments, likewise the 'Sermon on the Mount') must be seen from this soteriological point of view, that is, as making possible true freedom, life and salvation. 'Canon Law' also, if it is to be in accordance with the New Testament, cannot only ask for 'legitimisation', but must take seriously the 'soteriological intention' (apart from the social one) of rules and decrees. It cannot exactly be said that this has adequately taken place in the new CIC. At the same time one must distinguish between the self-justifying power of belief which brings man now in reality (ontologically speaking) to his true being, and the relative, provisional and changing ideas of order, salvation and humanity which always remain incomplete and more or less capable of improvement; one cannot argue away the difference between 'salvation', understood theologically, and 'well-being' in an earthly sense; that difference remains irrevocable. It is not a good idea to blur these dividing lines.

3. BRIEF 'FLASHBACK' TO THE 'EARTHLY JESUS'[15]

The Synoptic Gospels speak repeatedly of Jesus' *exousia*. In doing so, the word *exousia* appears with the following meanings: 1. the freedom and right to act, determine and dispose as one wishes; 2. the ability to act; as the potential, power and might to do so; in this way, listeners conclude from Jesus' teaching that He must have exousia (cf. Mark 1:22); 3. authority, absolute power, jurisdiction, authorisation.[16] Mark 1:22 describes the reaction of the crowd to Jesus' first appearance in the synagogue in Capernaum: 'They were astonished at his teaching, for he taught them as one who had authority, and not as their scribes' (see Matt. 7:23). Luke 4:32 says: '... for his word was the authority.' This editorial comment contrasts Jesus' teaching with that of the scribes. What the exact difference in content is, we never learn; only that Jesus' teaching is carried out with an 'authority' probably lacking in the teaching of the scribes. We are not mistaken if, in what Mark says, we think not only of the lack of any schooling or learning,[17] and similarly not only of Jesus' teaching alone, but also if we take into account the miracles, as is shown by the driving out of the demons which comes immediately afterwards (Mark 1:23–28). Following that the people repeat: 'a new teaching ... with authority' (Mark 1:27). Then the concept of 'authority' describes Jesus' outstanding ability to act which is manifest in all His work and teaching and, for that very reason, represents something quite different from the teaching of the scribes. In the story of the 'healing of the paralytic' (Mark 2:1–12) we read in Mark 2:10 (Matt. 9:6; Luke 5:24: the wording is taken over unchanged by the other two Gospel writers): '... But that you may know that the Son of man has authority/*exousia* on earth to forgive sins ...' Here it is not primarily a question of the forgiving of sins as practised by the Christian community—in New Testament times there was still no specific procedure for repentance, rather the forgiving of sins was principally connected with baptism—instead it is a question of the christological-soteriological authority of salvation in Jesus, the 'Son of man'. Jesus appears there as the sovereign representative of God, who, as 'Son of man', has the power on earth to carry out the forgiveness of sins which, according to the Judaic conception of God, is reserved for God 'in Heaven' alone.[18] In all of this we are dealing with the numinous, mysterious might of the totality of Jesus' work which can be felt in His words and deeds and cannot be put into any ready category. Jesus remains exalted, mysterious, unattainable; there is no basis on which one can come to terms with Him. These facts are corroborated exactly by Jesus likewise refusing to comply with the demand for a sign (see Mark 8:11–13) as a 'legitimisation' of His authority to cleanse the Temple (Mark 11:27–33).[19] This pericope is particularly instructive. The 'chief priests, scribes and elders' ask Jesus about His authority. Jesus counters this with the question: 'Was the baptism of John from heaven or from men?' To which the questioners reply: 'We do not know.' Jesus answers: 'Neither will I tell you by what authority I do these things.' Here again we see confirmed that Jesus' authority cannot be comprehended by the concept of 'legitimisation' or any 'yardstick of legitimisation'; there is no way of dealing with it. Rather it turns itself against the questioners who, in the final analysis, must themselves decide what their opinion is of Jesus and His message, whether they accept it or not. Jesus places man before the decisive question of belief. Beyond that, Jesus' authority is expressed in His conduct and His work, in such a way that man can experience its saving effect in himself (see 'John the Baptist's enquiry' Matt. 11:2–6, Luke 7:18–23).

4. DIAKONIA INSTEAD OF ARCHÉ[20]

The decisive factor in the New Testament understanding of the concepts 'power, sovereignty' etc., is that all exercise of power in Christ's Church is understood fundamentally as *diakonia* and not as *arché*. The concept of 'hierarchy' is not found in the New Testament, nor does 'the matter as such' arise. It is highly instructive that the word group *diakonia, diakonein* only appears marginally in the Septuagint (e.g. Esther 1:10; 2:2; 6:1–35; Proverbs 10:4; 1 Macc. 11:58; 4 Macc. 9:17) whereas the Hebrew *abd* and its derivatives are translated throughout by *douleuein, doulos*. On the other hand, this is never used in the New Testament to describe relationships of office and ministry within the Church, but rather for the relationship of believers and of the apostle to God or to the 'Lord Jesus Christ'. So Paul calls himself 'servant/minister of Jesus Christ, called to be an apostle' (Romans 1:1). The apostle stands in a mainly ministering relationship, as a servant towards his master. The semantic results are without doubt important, namely that instead of a relationship of superiority or inferiority we find another relationship, that of a willingness to minister to one's brothers and sisters on what is in the last analysis, a voluntary basis, and without deriving from this any ambitions or claims to status.

Without doubt, this new understanding of *diakonia* is grounded in the earthly Jesus, documented in what He says about 'ministering' (Mark 10:42–45; Matt. 20:25–28; see also Luke 22:25–27; John 13:1–17): 'You know that the rulers of the Gentiles lord it over them, and their great men exercise authority over them. It shall not be so among you; but whoever would be great among you must be your servant, and whosoever would be first among you must be your slave; even as the Son of man came not to be served but to serve, and to give his life as a ransom for many'. 'Ministry' of such a nature is not meant as a moral, inner attitude, but means far more, as the various christological-soteriological additions and developments show. Here it is a question of a fundamental understanding of the person of Jesus Himself; His whole existence together with His death on the Cross, appear to the Christian community as a 'ministry'. Jesus used the word 'ministry' not only in preaching to His disciples but He also took it very seriously on His own account, right up to His death on the Cross. If one also adds John's interpretation of the logion, the pericope of the 'washing of the feet' (John 13:1–17), then there emerges an impressive synthesis, determining the whole being and conduct of Jesus as a 'ministry', as a 'being for others', as the expression of the highest, most perfect love (John 13:1), as self-sacrifice that brings about salvation, thereby providing the ontological basis for the being of the Church and the Christian life.

The person to make *diakonia* the central concept of 'apostolic ministry' is the apostle Paul. So he asks the squabbling Corinthians: 'Who then is Paul, and who is Apollos?', giving the immediate answer: 'ministers by whom ye believed' (1 Cor. 3:5). The 'ministry' of Paul consists in his especial calling as 'apostle to the heathen' whose task is to bring the Gospel to the peoples of the world. Paul also calls this service to the Gospel 'ministry of the spirit', or 'ministry of righteousness or justification', in contrast to 'ministry of death and condemnation' which took place, according to Paul, in Jewish devoutness under the Law (cf. 2 Cor. 3:7–11). It is also a ministry of liberation, leading to freedom. Lastly the apostolic ministry is a 'ministry of reconciliation' (2 Cor. 5:17–20), and indeed not only within the Christian community, for the Gospel proclaims the reconciliation of the world wrought by God Hismelf: 'And All this is from God, who through Christ reconciled us to himself and gave us the ministry of reconciliation: that is, in Christ God was reconciling the world to himself …' (2 Cor. 5:18–19). The Gospel, Christians, the Christian community and the ecclesiastical office must, according to this Pauline concept, represent in the world and for the world the decisive 'power of reconciliation' against all powers dividing God and the world.

In 1 Thess. 2:1–16, the apostle describes his own conduct as exemplary *diakonia* from which can be seen, as it were, how 'apostolic ministry' appears in practice in the community (cf. also 1 Cor. 9:1–13). But the goal of the apostolic ministry' is 'the responsible community'[21] and also the 'organisation of the community' (see 1 Cor. 14). The Pauline ideal of the Christian community does not consist in making believers dependent on the ecclesiastical office, but in assisting them towards their own responsibility and independence as self-accountable Christians (see 1 Cor. 3:1–4)! In addition, what is said about the 'Body of Christ' (1 Cor. 12:1–3, 4–11, 12–31; Rom. 12:4ff.), taken together with what is said about spiritual gifts, is present in the ministry of responsibility, freedom and the greatest possible self-accountability of Christian communities. In using the image of the 'Body of Christ', the apostle is at pains to make clear the relationship between unity and diversity, between variety and interaction or reciprocity in the community. All the body's limbs are necessary in their place; no limb may make itself or its function absolute at the expense of other limbs and their tasks as if it were the whole body; there is here no kind of uniformity or claim to monopoly. In addition, Paul introduces another criterion: 'To each is given manifestation of the Spirit for the common good, *pros to sympheron*' (1 Cor. 12:7). Paul's great achievement, which still concerns us today, lies in his recognition of the exceptional quality of spiritual gifts in every respect—Paul is in no way an opponent of charisms!—and in his perception of the need at the same time to draw their fangs of egotism and self-interest, by committing these gifts to the *bonum commune* of the physical community. Using the First Epistle to the Corinthians as an example, one could in general demonstrate comprehensively what one's dealings with the Christian community should be like, if one understands them seriously from the viewpoint of the basic idea of *diakonia*.

In conclusion we can perhaps say that 'ministry' as well as 'authority', to be understood in their jesuanic-christological-soteriological connection, as well as in conjunction with their theological background (God as Father, as absolute love), and also bearing in mind the general Pauline interpretation— this is the 'authority of love'. By that we do not mean something purely sentimental in the midst of an otherwise rather brutal world, but rather something very exact, simple, practical and genuinely concrete. Love as *agape/caritas* is the ability or power to help another or others to their own being and to their ability to achieve that being. Real authority is rendered superfluous. This is something great and can in no way be taken for granted. But that may be precisely the point.

Translated by Gordon Wood

Notes

1. See R. Guardini *Die Macht* (Würzburg 1951).
2. On this whole question see Th. Eschenburg *Über Autorität* (edition suhrkamp 129, Frankfurt a. M. 1965).
3. Quoted according to Hugo Rahner *Kirche und Staat im frühen Christentum* (Munich 1961) 256f.
4. See G. Van Der Leeuw *Phänomenologie der Religion* (Tübingen [2]1956) who in general takes the concept of power as his starting point §§ 1–4; for quotations see 33.
5. See the interpretation by W. Trilling *Das wahre Israel* (Munich 1964, 'Der Inhalt des Manifestes 28, 18–20', 21–51); slightly different now in A. Sand, 'Das Evangelium nach Matthäus', *RNT 1*, (Regensburg 1986, 594–604; 'Ein Zentralbegriff der Perikope ist der von der 'exousia' (Macht, Vollmacht), die von Gott dem Auferweckten verliehen ist', 599).
6. Trilling *Das wahre Israel*, 50.
7. Still a standard text E. Lohmeyer *Kyrios Jesus. Eine Untersuchung zu Phil 2,5–11* (1927/28—reprint Darmstadt 1961). As it is not possible or even necessary at this point to quote the extensive literature on this text, I refer readers to the good interpretation and discussion in J. Gnilka *Der Philipperbrief* HTK X/3 (Freiburg-Basel-Vienna [2]1976, 111–131—interpretation); on that theme see 'Exkurs 3: Das vorpaulinische Christuslied' 131–147.
8. On the whole question of the origin and meaning of the kyrios title with reference to Jesus: W. Bousset *Kyrios Christos* (1st edition 1913, Göttingen [5]1965); O. Cullmann *Die Christologie des Neuen Testaments* (Tübingen 1957) III. Teil: 'Die auf das gegenwärtige Werk Jesu bezüglichen christologischen Titel', 1. Kapitel: Jesus der Herr, 199–244; F. Hahn *Christologische Hoheitstitel* (Göttingen 1963, § 2. Kyrios, 67–132; W. Kramer 'Christo-Kyrios-Gottessohn' (*AThANT 44*, Zürich 1963); G. Quell/W. Foerster 'Kyrios' (*ThWNT III*, 1038–1098); C. U. Dodd *According to the Scriptures* (Digswell Place reprint 1961).

9. Contrast G. Hasenhüttl *Herrschaftsfreie Kirche* (Düsseldorf 1974) who completely disregards the christological-soteriological basic structure of the 'sovereignty of Jesus Christ'.

10. See on this theme W. Trilling *Das wahre Israel*, 40ff.

11. See K.-H. Ohlig *Fundamentalchristologie* (Munich 1986).

12. Trilling *Das wahre Israel*, 41. See also J. Blank 'Jesus—die Gegenwart Gottes in der Geschichte' in his *Christliche Orientierungen* (Düsseldorf 1981) 129–139.

13. Billerbeck I, 794 on Matt. 18:20 gives numerous instances.

14. See J. Blank *Krisis* (Freiburg i.Br., 1964) Chap. 3, John 5:19–30: 'Die christologisch-eschatologische Vergegenwärtigungstheologie des Johannes', 109–182.

15. On this section see J. Blank 'Die Vollmacht der Liebe' in his *Das Evangelium als Garantie der Freiheit*, 57–78.

16. See W. Bauer *Griechisch-Deutsches Wörterbuch* (Berlin [5]1963 Col. 550f.); W. Foerster 'exousia' in *ThWNT* II, 559–571.

17. On Jewish schooling as it might well have been at the time of Jesus, see E. Schürer *Geschichte des Jüdischen Volkes im Zeitalter Jesu Christi II* (reprint Hildesheim 1964, 333ff. § 25) (= *The History of the Jewish People in the Age of Jesus Christ vol II* Edinburgh, 1979,p. 25, 314–380); G. Stemberger *Das klassische Judentum* (Munich 1979, II.E. 'Das Schulwesen', 109–125); J. Blank 'Lernprozesse im Jüngerkreis' *ThQ* 158 (1978), 163–177.

18. On this see J. Blank 'Weißt du, was Versöhnung heißt? Der Kreuztod Jesu als Sühne und Versöhnung' in: J. Blank/J. Werbick *Sühne und Versöhnung/Theologie zur Zeit* 1 (Düsseldorf 1986, 21–91, 59f.).

19. On this see J. Gnilka 'Das Evangelium nach Markus (Mark 8; 27–16,20)' *EKK II/2* (Zürich, Neukirchen-Vluyn 1979, 136–141); R. Pesch 'Das Markusevangelium II. Teil' *HTK II/2* (Freiburg, Basel, Vienna 1977, 208–213); 'Die Perikope macht die theologische und humane Dimension ernsthafter Frage nach der Autorität des Anspruches Jesu klar', 212.

20. On this see my comprehensive essay 'Mitarbeiter an eurer Freude. Vom Stil des kirchlichen Amtes' in *Gemeinde ohne Priester—Kirche ohne Zukunft* (Verlag J. Knecht, Frankfurt a. M., 1983, 9–56) also reprinted in J. Blank *Vom Urchristentum zur Kirche* (Munich 1982, 174–218). See also W. Beyer 'diakoneo', etc. in *ThWNT II*, 81–93.

21. See K. Maly *Mündige Gemeinde* (Stuttgart 1967).

John E. Lynch

Power in the Church: an Historico-critical Survey

IN EXAMINING the exercise of power, one must be aware of two closely related concepts, influence and authority. 'It is by now a fairly well established hypothesis that concepts shape (if they do not wholly determine) perception.'[1] The three concepts often used interchangeably are not truly congruent—even if there is not agreement on the precise nature of the distinctions. There are certainly different connotations in describing someone as 'powerful' or 'influential' or as 'having authority'. For purposes of this survey it seems fruitful to consider *authority* as the right to command, *power* (which may or may not coincide with authority) as the achievement or control of intended effects, and *influence* as an indirect or moral control. From this perspective five periods of church history will be investigated.

THE PRIMITIVE CHURCH

By the end of the first century some Christian communities continued to be governed by a collegial group on the model of the Jewish synagogue while others had a single overseer. The various charisms spoken of by St Paul were gradually being institutionalised. In the *Didache*, for example, the liturgical duties formerly reserved to the prophets and teachers are in the process of being subsumed by overseers and deacons (10:7; 15:1–2). The letters of Ignatius of Antioch present the final stage of development: the single overseer or bishop who presides over the liturgy and teaches, the council of elders who rule with the bishop, and the deacons who look after practical concerns. The three offices taken together comprise a unity; without them the name 'Church' is not given (Trallians 3:1). Repeatedly the community is exhorted to 'do nothing without the bishop' (Phil. 7:2) and to be 'submissive to the elders' (Trallians 2:2).

One very good reason why the community should respect its leaders is that the people have chosen them. The Acts of the Apostles records that the whole assembly participated in the selection of Matthias (1:15–26) and also in the choice of 'the seven' after the Hellenist dispute (6:1–6). The popular election of officials thus became a paradigm for the early Church. In time the neighbouring bishops will have the dominant voice, but still the wishes of the people must be respected. Pope Celestine I in a letter to the bishops of Gaul (c. 425) insists that no bishop is to be imposed on a congregation unwilling to receive him (Eph. 4:5). Pope Leo the Great a few years later reiterated the principle: the bishop who is to be placed over all should be elected by all (Eph. 10).

The bishop did not rule autocratically but in collegial fashion with his presbytery. The ordination prayer for the presbyter in the *Apostolic Tradition* stresses the corporate character of the presbyterate and its special grace of counsel. The bishop prays that the ordinand share in the presbyterate and govern thy people (n. 8:2). At the beginning of his episcopate (c. 249) Cyprian writes to his presbyters and deacons: 'I have decided to do nothing of my own opinion privately without your advice and the consent of the people' (Eph. 14:4).

Though the bishop and his presbyters hold real authority, they are answerable to the local church which at the time was largely autonomous and self-sufficient. Ecclesial policy was set at home. When the bishop went to a synod, he did so as the representative of his people. Any decision of the bishops was not imposed on the local community but had first to be ratified by them. The problems of administration that come with large organisations and the competition of State and society had yet to be faced.

THE POST-CONSTANTINIAN AGE

The conversion of the Emperor Constantine led to profound changes in ecclesial life. The emperor was very much part of an absolutist tradition. Roman religion had long been a responsibility of state, publicly maintained to secure divine favour; the emperor was *pontifex maximus*. As a Christian Constantine quite understandably retained this attitude. He considered himself 'bishop for external affairs' of the Church. In the East, especially, no one thought to challenge these assumptions. The new atmosphere of benevolence was in such stark contrast to the period of persecution that it could be attributed only to divine providence. Besides, it was not a question of outside interference because the emperor was himself the most prominent member of the Church.

Churchmen were only too willing to accept imperial largess and even sought help in enforcing purely religious decisions. Within months of the Edict of Toleration they appealed to Constantine in the Donatist dispute and he eventually summoned the Council of Arles in 314; a momentous precedent was thus established in Church-State religions. It will be the emperor who will convoke the seven ecumenical councils of antiquity, the only ones recognised by both East and West.

Until the fall of the empire in 1453 the emperor exerted enormous power in the Eastern Church. He had the duty of promoting orthodoxy, not in the sense of determining the faith but of implementing concilar decisions. 'He also legislated freely in disciplinary and administrative matters affecting the Church, and on occasion against the will of Patriarch and metropolitans.'[2] He was called the 'living' or 'animate law', *empsychos nomos* (Novel 105) and the twelfth-century canonist Balsamon went so far as to imply that the emperor was above canon law.

To be able to cope with the state on a more equal footing, the Church had to develop an organisational structure beyond the local level. The province or eparchy and the patriarchate quickly curtained diocesan independence of the previous era. No longer would a bishop with his presbyters and people decide policy at home but in distant councils with his fellow bishops. Their decisions would be imposed locally without regard for particular customs. Instead of representing authority *within his community*, the bishop began to represent a far-removed, impersonal synodal authority *to that community*. The intimate bond between the bishop and his people loosened. The people lost their voice in his selection (earlier in the East than in the West). The leader who used to be considered wedded to his church could now be transferred without regard for its wishes.

The need for the Church to negotiate with a worldwide empire greatly accelerated the development of a universal ecclesiastical power, the papacy. The bishop or Rome has asserted primatial leadership as early as the second century when Pope Victor (c. 190) during a dispute over the celebration of Easter threatened to excommunicate the dioceses of Asia. For the most part, however, there was little occasion for the pope to exercise any universalist function in the pre-Nicene Church. Circumstances were completely different over the next two centuries. The pressure of political events and the great doctrinal controversies roused the popes to vindicate their primatial claims. Pope Damasus (366–384), for instance, to emphasise his unique position began to speak of Rome as the 'Apostolic See' and to address the bishops as 'sons' rather than the customary 'brothers'. Pope Leo the Great (440–464) sought juridical control over all the churches: he orders, decides, reprehends, deposes, corrects, defines—the language of one who possesses the *gubernacula ecclesiae universalis*.[3]

THE CAROLINGIAN EPOCH

At the very time Leo the Great was so vigorously asserting papal power, imperial rule in the West crumbled under waves of barbarian assault. Church organisation dependent upon the municipal structure of the empire atrophied with the slow disintegration of urban life. Fortunately, there arose a new lay movement well adapted to survive in the changed environment. Monasticism proved to be the most powerful force in Christianity from the fifth to the eleventh centuries. It began apart from and sometimes opposed to the institutional church but at the Council of Chalcedon in 451 received official recognition. In certain rural areas, like Ireland, the Church came to be organised around the monastery where the abbot, usually not a bishop, exercised jurisdiction. The essential connection between the episcopal order and ecclesial government was thereby obscured. By virtue of their ascetic and contemplative lives the monks wielded vast influence. Considered bearers of spiritual power, they were sought out for direction and played a role analogous to that of the charismatics in primitive Christianity. The Celtic monks, in fact, were completely responsible for revamping penitential discipline.

The collapse of imperial rule left the Italian peninsula prey to the incursions of the Lombards. In desperation the popes turned for protection to the Franks who were emerging as the most formidable power in the West. Charlemagne, the Frankish king crowned Roman Emperor on Christmas day in the year 800, was no less anxious than the emperors of the past to bring the Church under his tutelage. He wrote Pope Leo III that it was the pope's duty to pray and the emperor's to direct the external affairs of the Church. In his capitularies he legislated on almost every aspect of ecclesiastical life.

To unify his vast domain which comprised most of Western Europe, Charlemagne embarked on a campaign of Christianisation, which for him meant the religion practised at Rome. Having obtained from the papacy authentic copies of the liturgy, the canon law and the Benedictine monastic rule, he attempted to impose them everywhere. From that time onward in the West *Christianitas* became virtually indistinguishable from *Romanitas*. One unfortunate result was to make lay participation negligible, in so far as Latin was for the non-cleric an unknown tongue.

The spiritual and temporal were so intermingled in Carolingian Europe that bishops functioned more as officers of the State than as ecclesiatics. Since at the beginning of the period at least the clergy comprised the educated class, they were coopted into government service to the detriment of their pastoral duties. A further confusion of secular and spiritual interests were the *Eigenkirchen* or privately owned churches. According to Germanic law one who built a church on his land retained complete control over it, appointing and removing clergy at will. Ownership of church buildings was conveyed along with the title to the land. Monastic churches were also proprietary churches. By the ninth century the number of such churches vastly outnumbered the episcopal churches. The effect on the power of the diocesan bishop was disastrous.

The encroachment of lay power was to continue unabated. In the century after Charlemagne the conception of the proprietary church would be applied to bishoprics and abbeys as it had been to lesser churches. Under the new legal theory kings and magnates exercised full dominion over them. Bishoprics and abbeys began to be conferred in the form of an *enfeoffment,* a solemn act later known as investiture. The papacy itself did not escape depredation at the hands of a predatory aristocracy for a century and a half (896–1048). The power of the nobility over the Church seemed complete.

THE GREGORIAN REFORM

Meanwhile, movements of reform were stirring in the monasteries of Burgundy (Cluny), Lorraine, and northern Italy. At length the German Emperor Henry III intervened to free the papacy and a new epoch dawned for the Church. It is called the Gregorian Reform after its dominant figure Pope Gregory VII (1073–1085) who embarked on a programme to free the Church from lay domination. The revivified papacy had such prestige that he could excommunicate Emperor Henry IV and threaten to depose him. The papacy won a victory in principle though imperial encroachment was not wholly eliminated. As a result of the reform lay power in the Church would henceforth be regarded with suspicion and resisted. When election of bishops was restored it did not revert to the clergy and people but was restricted to the cathedral chapters.

From the viewpoint of power distribution in the Church the most significant feature of the Gregorian programme was the inauguration of a policy of Roman centralisation not to be reversed until the Second Vatican

Council. The *Dictatus papae* of Gregory VII lists twenty-seven papal prerogatives. To the Apostolic See are to be referred the more important matters of every church. The Roman pontiff alone can transfer, depose or reinstate bishops, make laws for the whole church, divide and unite dioceses and erect new abbacies.

The papacy in the twelfth century gradually acquired the right to confirm the election of all metropolitans. The most significant advance in papal control was jurisdiction over disputed elections which soon led to the simple confirmation of suffragan bishoprics. The traditional formula 'bishops by the grace of God' was expanded to include 'and of the Apostolic See'. As the thirteenth century progressed the confirmation of bishops was transformed on an increasing scale to direct appointment.

If the pope was becoming an absolute monarch in the Western Church, the bishop was becoming an autocrat in the diocese. The revival of Roman law in the twelfth century fostered the notion of absolutism. The clergy were not considered his co-adjutors but his subjects. When the bishop went on a visitation, he did so as a judge rather than a shepherd. His court was a resort for litigants, a tribunal to punish spiritual offences. Canonists referred to a pastor 'governing' his parish instead of 'serving' or caring for the people. From top to bottom the Church had evolved into a quasi-state of the most authoritative kind.[4]

Though not participating in government or jurisdiction, the newly established university system, like monasticism before it, began about the year 1200 to influence church life on a large scale. The universities came close to constituting an independent order as Alexander of Roes recognised about 1281: 'By these three, namely, the priesthood, the empire, and the university [*studium*] the holy Catholic church is spiritually sustained, increased, and ruled as by three virtues. ...'[5] Even though in theory created by the papacy, the universities did not always heed its directives. Aristotelianism, for example, despite episcopal and papal prohibition flourished in centres of higher learning throughout Europe. The universities were represented at the Council of Constance (1414–18) where doctors of canon law and theology very likely voted with the prelates as they did in the previous councils of Pisa (1409) and Rome (1412–13).

The Council of Constance, regarded as the sixteenth ecumenical council, has the undeniable distinction of settling the Great Western Schism. The council enacted two very controversial decrees: (1) *Haec sancta*, declaring that the council derived its authority immediately from God and that the pope owed obedience to it; (2) *Frequens*, obliging the pope to summon councils at specific intervals. *Haec sancta* is not dogmatic teaching but a legal enactment; it does not determine the relation of papal and conciliar power, as extreme conciliarists would maintain, but the procedure to be followed in an emergency situation.

The success of Constance in ending the Great Western Schism led many to believe that the danger of another schism precipitated by the sixteenth-century reformers could be headed off by a general council. Luther almost immediately appealed over the head of the pope to such a forum. His admission, however, during the Leipzig debate of 1519, that a council could err (as Constance did in condemning John Huss) more than the ninety-five theses of two years earlier or even his excommunication two years later initiated Luther's Reformation.[6] This admission brought home to Luther and his opponents the extent of alienation between him and the Roman Church. When the papacy finally overcame its fears of conciliarism and summoned the Council of Trent (1545–63), the time for healing had passed. No Protestants attended any of its sessions.

The Reformation had plummeted on an irreversible fissiparous course. Once the reformers set up the Bible as the ultimate authority, they had no convincing argument to those who read the Bible and came to conclusions different from their own. In practice, the established church in a particular country backed up by the secular arm had the last word.

In all European countries, as a result of the dissolution of the one supra-national Church, princes gained inordinate power over their churches. The reform decrees of Trent, for instance, were never published for the Empire as a whole or officially promulgated in France. As late as the election of Pius X in 1903 Austria claimed the right to veto one candidate in a papal election. Spain and France had also demanded this *jus exclusivae*. Spain did not renounce its privilege of presenting candidates to vacant episcopal sees until 1976.

After the Reformation the need for Catholics to close ranks and speak with one voice greatly enhanced papal power. Though Trent was unable to resolve the hotly debated theological question whether the episcopal power of jurisdiction came immediately from God or mediately through the Roman pontiff, it did leave many important practical matters to the personal disposition of the papacy: revised editions of the Bible, the missal and the breviary; a profession of faith; a catechism; and an index of prohibited books. These responsibilities led to the complete reorganisation and expansion of the Roman Curia. The Sacred Congregation of the Council was established to interpret authentically the decrees of Trent; no commentaries or glosses could be published without its approval. The power of the bishops, nonetheless, was strengthened within their dioceses. The medieval practice of exemption whereby monasteries, religious, and chapters of cathedrals were withdrawn from episcopal authority had led in many instances to a state of religious anarchy. The council gave the right of supervision over these exempt bodies to the bishops, not by virtue of their own episcopal jurisdiction, but as permanent delegates of the Apostolic See. The council also restored to the diocesan bishops much of their power that had been eroded through the rise of the archdeacon who could judge matrimonial and criminal cases.

In the centuries after Trent centralisation of power continued to accelerate. The reorganisation of the Roman Curia in 1587 canonised the congregation system of government. 'This meant that centralisation became bureaucratic; and the cardinals in the Curia became an oligarchy which in a collegial way (*collegium cardinalium*) governed the Church with the pope.'[7] The expanded papal nunciatures kept the bishops under surveillance, promoted the implementation of curial directives, and guarded against innovations. The emphasis on papal authority culminated in the declaration at the First Vatican Council (1870) that the definitions of the Roman pontiff are irreformable *ex sese, non autem ex consensu ecclesiae*.[8] In 1917 Code of Canon Law was the legal embodiment of that council, upholding that the Church is basically monarchical in structure. The Roman pontiff has full and supreme power of jurisdiction over the whole Church. Episcopal jurisdiction is limited to the diocese. Patriarchs, metropolitans, regional and provincial synods participate in delegated papal authority rather than exercise episcopal power.

The Second Vatican Council reversed the policy of centralisation which had been in effect since the time of the Gregorian reform. Instead of a monarchical structure the Church is seen to be a hierarchical communion with the pope at its head. Even when speaking of the pope's infallibility, the Council refers to him as head of the college of bishops (*Lumen gentium* n. 25). All jurisdiction is essentially episcopal (n. 22); it has the same source as orders, namely, episcopal consecration (n. 21).

The 1983 Code has canonised conciliar teaching. The college of bishops whose head is the Supreme Pontiff has supreme and full power over the universal Church (c. 336). Episcopal conferences are constituted of all the bishops of a country or certain territory (c. 447). The principle of subsidiarity is recognised in so far as the conferences have real though limited authority (c. 455, § 1). A diocesan bishops has all the ordinary, proper, and immediate power required for carrying out his pastoral office (c. 381). He can dispense from the universal law in disciplinary matters, except for certain reserved cases (c. 87, § 1). The bishop is to use his authority in a spirit of coresponsibility, consulting with the presbyteral council (c. 495), the diocesan pastoral council (c. 511), and the finance council (493). The clergy and laity may be consulted in the selection of bishops (c. 377, § 3). Where there is a shortage of priests, the laity may be entrusted with a share in the exercise of the pastoral care of a parish (c. 517, § 2). The laity can cooperate (*cooperari possunt*) in the exercise of the power of government or jurisdiction.

CONCLUSION

No human community can prosper without authority and power. Therefore, Christ 'instituted in his Church a variety of ministries ... endowed with sacred power.' He willed that the successors of the Apostles, namely the bishops, 'together with the successors of Peter, the visible head of the whole Church, govern the house of the living God' (*Lumen gentium* n. 18). The government of the Church has functioned through a variety of structures in the course of history. It has adopted features of the feudal state, the absolute monarchical state, the army and the corporation. The administrative structure, however, is not authority but the instrument of authority.

Similarly ecclesiastical authority must not identify itself with the will of God; otherwise self-criticism is impossible. At Vatican II Paul VI and the Decree on Ecumenism (n. 3) frankly acknowledged that the Catholic Church was partly to blame for schisms. In honesty authority must be prepared to admit mistakes; it must also be ready to abide by contemporary standards of justice. It is not clear, for instance, that canon law gives adequate recognition to the principle of due process that has been constitutionalised in secular society.

In the world today public opinion, even in non-democratic societies is a potent force influencing government policies just as in the past agencies without power or authority such as the monastery and the university profoundly affected the direction of the Church. New strategies must be developed to give the laity a meaningful voice in Church affairs. Despite the efforts of Vatican II, the Church still appears to be a pyramid with all power flowing from the top down. Authority whose purpose is to serve must be open to those who are being served.

Notes

1. D. V. J. Bell *Power, Influence, and Authority: an Essay in Political Linguistics* (New York 1975), 5.

2. J. M. Hussey *The Orthodox Church in the Byzantine Empire* (Oxford 1986), p. 302.

3. W. Ullmann 'Leo I and the Theme of Papal Primacy', *Journal of Theological*

Studies 11 (1960) 25. *Gubernaculum* in fifth-century language is not 'government' but the rudder of the [ship of] the Church—quite a different emphasis.

4. T. M. Parker 'Feudal Episcopacy', *The Aposotolic Ministry*, ed. K. E. Kirk (London 1962), p. 381.

5. H. Rashdall *The Universities of Europe in the Middle Ages* (London 1936) I, p. 23. Also see G. Leff *Paris and Oxford Universities in the Thirteenth and Fourteenth Centuries* (New York 1968), p. 3.

6. J. Pelikan *Obedient Rebels: Catholic Substance and Protestant Principle in Luther's Reformation* (New York 1964), p. 54.

7. R. E. McNally 'The Tridentine Church: a Study in Ecclesiology,' *Law for Liberty: the Role of Law in the Church Today*, ed. J. Biechler (Baltimore 1967), p. 75.

8. Sessio IV, 18 July 1970, Caput IV (COD, 792).

Eric Fuchs

Sex and Power in the Church

IN THE early Church 'sex became a factor with a highly symbolic loading precisely because its extinction was deemed a possibility in a committed individual, and because it was thought that this extinction would disclose the qualities required of the director of a religious community, and do so more meaningfully than any other transformation of a human being'.[1] Historical studies, therefore, confirm that, from the remotest antiquity, power in the Church has accrued to those who overcome sex itself in order to withstand the trials which people have to undergo because of sex. There are various reasons for this association of sex and power. Essentially, they may be subsumed under two models.

First: power belongs to the person who can offer the example of unyielding discipline in this respect. Celibacy and chastity are imposed on the clergy, so that they in their turn can guide and improve the moral standards of lay sexual behaviour. This model is western rather than eastern and appeared very soon in the early Church. It is an ascetic tendency which seeks to impose moral norms on sex by placing it within the precise bounds of a restrictive discipline.[2] An extreme reversion to the theory of the pagan moralists, this ethic would force all Christian existence to submit to the demands of communitarian witness. It is absolutely necessary to avoid the risk of offending against the Christian ideal of fraternal communion which claims to do away with social, political and sexual forms of determinism. That, however, means supervising believers' conduct, all the more so since, in this area above all, they are besmirched by the sin of concupiscence. From Tertullian to Augustine, a disciplinary ethos evolved in which mistrust of sexuality grew simultaneously with the power of the celibate clergy. They had found an extreme solution to the problem by renouncing marriage, and by choosing the unifying path of

23

chastity. Moreover, 'in our age it is better from all viewpoints, and holier, not to seek out for oneself a carnal form of self-perpetuation, but to preserve oneself forever from all marital bonds, and to submit spiritually to Christ, one's only spouse'.[3] Thereafter, the celibate clergy had the right to guide their lay brethren, who were weaker because they had accepted the concupiscence ineluctably associated with marriage. What is more, they were entitled to make the laity aware of the serious moral implications of sex.

Second: the other model aims to interiorise the relationship with sex to the point of mastering it completely, and banishing even its most tenacious effects to the realm of the believer's imagination, or unconscious. This above all was the monastic solution, the way of recovery of the original man, the Adam of paradise who lived close to God and free of sex and desire. From Gregory of Nyssa to John Cassian and Evagrius, a vast company of spiritual mentors appeared who subjected themselves to impassibility, for 'the Kingdom of heaven is impassibility of the soul, and the true science of beings'.[4]

In this case, sex is not so much determined and controlled as denied. It is reduced to the level of a mere symptom indicating the existence of other, much more deadly passions. It is denied as an anomaly which a spiritual person can master by reducing it to insignificance. As John Cassian says: '... it means leaving the flesh while remaining in the body; overcoming nature rather than living in the fragility of the flesh while dwelling in the body; and overcoming nature rather than living in the fragility of the flesh without fleeing its torments'.[5] 'This means overcoming nature (*ultra naturam esse*) in order to recover the 'protological' image of man in his primal state,[6] unblemished by sin. The man who attains to this total mastery is acknowledged as a spiritual master. But the very radical nature of such a venture means that it can be managed only by especially estimable people, who are all the more admirable because they are so exceptional. Their authority on a spiritual level is certainly considerable, but their power on the moral level remains limited. It was not long before two moralities became possible in the East: either one left the world for the desert, or one married in order to lead a conjugal life that was as free from problems of sexuality as possible. The monastic ideal ensured great prestige for those who were capable of it, and it did not disqualify those who God allowed to experience their sexuality within the framework of marriage.

The second model prevailed in the East, whereas the disciplinary model became dominant in the West. There the connection between sin and sexual behaviour was stressed, as it had been as early as Augustine. Before long clerics were professionally esteemed in terms of their ability to assess the degree of wickedness of sexual acts. This establishment during the Middle Ages of a legal and disciplinary morality was paralleled by the long struggle in the western Church to impose celibacy on the clergy. Breaking with the old tradition retained in the East, and reaffirmed by the so-called Quinisextual Council of 692, which authorised married priests, and in spite of much resistance and the serious moral disadvantages of the practice, the Catholic Church closely associated the exercise of power in the Church with a denigration of sex. To make it effective, this link had to be concealed symbolically.[7] At first, to be sure, it was a matter of the cleric embodying the norm, but that is a fragile position since it makes power dependent on the authority of whomsoever affirms the norm and has to submit to it before anyone else. Power had to be secured apart from this exemplary morality, on unquestionable—in other words, sacred—foundations. Hence the link was established between celibacy and purity. This was a ritual purity before it was moral, and it ensured the priest's possession of ontological superiority; it was based on an outdated notion of sex as defilement, and therefore as something irreconcilable with the celebration of the Eucharist. 'At the start of the canonical tradition from which the law of celibacy in the West derives, we find the law of 'eucharistic continence', which forbade sexual relations on the night before communion'.[8] This argument linking celibacy with the service of the altar reappeared in an encyclical of Pius XII *Sacra virginitas* of 1954.[9] It had travelled the entire history of the Catholic Church from the Council of Elvira (306); this indicates its strength, which is of a symbolic character. Henceforth the awful sacred realm of sex was countered by the reassuring holy domain of the asexual fraternity of the Eucharist, celebrated by priests quite unsullied by sex.

I shall not examine the anthropological significance of this kind of reduction of sexuality to impurity,[10] but merely remark that it means the establishment of a strict system of behavioural control, founded both on the sacred character of the guardians of the Law, and on the advantages of the disciplinary rules which they pronounced in order to preserve believers from the threat of the sexual taboo.

By reinforcing fear of sex in this way, the ecclesiastical institution reinforced its own power, for it alone, through its clergy, was able to put right the vile consequences of this ontological deficiency. It adjusted this state of affairs through the practice of penitence, the ecclesiastical ministry of reconciliation which, as Pierre Legendre says, supposed 'an exchange of sin for punishment',[11] and by laying down the rules meticulously. A new figure appeared—no longer that of the spiritual master or the ethical model, but the consecrated figure of the castrated father. In the image of the Pope whose power he represented, the priest was the bearer of the Law and yet devoid of sexual capacity. His was a threatening figure, for he was able to say what was licit and what illicit, yet he was also reassuring, for he represented a living solution of the dilemma (how to be a father, a pope, without sex).

In a system of this kind, the setting apart of the clergy, grounded on the major prohibition represented by the rule of continence, was the condition and sign of a power as exercised over a laity treated as minors. In the course of the Middle Ages theologians tried to revalue marriage,[12] yet in spite of the resistance of numerous trends to obligatory celibacy within the Catholic Church,[13] the Council of Trent solemnly reaffirmed that virginity was superior to the married state: 'If anyone says that marriage should precede virginity or celibacy, and it is not better or holier to remain in a state of virginity or celibacy, rather than to be united in marriage, let him be anathema' (Can. 9). Thus it maintained the bipartite status of clergy—superior because continent—and laity—inferior because subject to the impurity of 'the law of sin inherited through the genital parts', as a medieval text puts it.[14] Of course these two estates ensured the operation of the rules of power. The hierarchical ecclesiology imposed in the Roman Catholic Church relied on this antithetical relation between the realm of the religious sacred and the (bad) domain of the sexual sacred.

The Reformation rejected this system. It directly pronounced against priestly celibacy, the sacred character of the priesthood, and the temporal power of the Church. The Reformers questioned the immorality of priestly celibacy as it was lived in the sixteenth century, and thus in fact attacked the very structure of power in the western Church. By opposing the material power of the Church which obscured the sole acceptable authority of Holy Scripture, they very soon began to question monastic vows and obligatory celibacy. There is a direct link between that and the rejection of a division of Christians into clergy and laity. The rising lay awareness at the end of the Middle Ages was actually burst forth as it were, in the Reformation. Indeed, in this perspective priestly celibacy seemed the very symbol of a refusal to acknowledge the importance and maturity of the laity.

That is why the Reformers' fundamental arguments against compulsory celibacy always appealed to freedom of conscience. 'As to the prohibition of the marriage of priests, I say that it manifests a wicked tyranny, not only against the Word of God, but against all equity. First, it was never permissible for men to forbid what God had placed within the bounds of our freedom of choice. Second, it is notorious, and needs no demonstration, that our Lord expressly ordained that this freedom should not be constrained in any way'.[15] Nothing which God had 'placed within the bounds of our freedom of choice' could be forbidden, even by the Church. In order to stress the value of the lay condition, the Reformers' teaching exalted the value of marriage: 'Our Lord Jesus Christ so honoured marriage that he pronounced it the image and sign of the holy and sacred unity which he enjoyed with the Church. What more could be said to uphold the dignity of marriage? How impudent therefore to say that it is unclean and polluted, when it discloses the spiritual grace of Jesus Christ?'[16]

Here power passes from the one who shut himself off from sexual capacity to the one who assumes it as a vocation with heavy moral responsibility. The figure of the castrated father is replaced by that of the father of the lay family, the authentic model of all authority, political, ecclesiastical or professional. Moreover, this figure, inasmuch as it acknowledged its sexuality, presupposed a new relation to women. They were no longer saved by chastity or motherhood; instead womanhood was authentically signified by the marital state.[17] Man's companion—though of course his inferior—a woman not only realised herself in marriage but enabled a man to realise himself in the marital couple, which henceforth became the basic unit of Church and society. Power belonged to the father of a family, but by definition he could be one only by forming a couple together with a woman. That was the start of the process which has led to contemporary Protestantism allowing women to be ordained as ministers of the Word.

By exalting the figure of the father of a family, the Reformation was far from resolving all difficulties. In our sense, it should be praised for making the problem more obvious. Henceforth, as Molière says, 'the supreme power was on the male side'. The man/woman relationship became central once again, as it is in Scripture, whereas it is wholly obscured in the priestly system, where the antithesis is before all else one of clergy/laity. With the Reformation, the truth which had been concealed by the heavy and pedantic discourse of casuistry reappeared: the sex and power relationship is essentially that between man and woman.

In our own age, however, this problem has been directly posed because of the growing awareness among women of their past subjection. This consciousness is also associated with the revaluation of sex as an area within which otherness may be acknowledged. Therefore it must call in question any system which would ground its power on the exclusion of this dimension of otherness. How long will it be before ears are opened to the question posed by the women in our Churches who want an end to a power game based solely on their denial as women? Are we on the eve of another reformation?

Translated by J. G. Cumming

Notes

1. P. Brown *Histoire de la vie privée*, Vol. I, ch. 2: 'Antiquité tardive' (Paris 1985) 257.

2. E. Fuchs *Le Désir et la tendresse. Sources et histoire d'une ethique chrétienne de la sexualité et du mariage* (Geneva 1986) 81–89.

3. Augustine *De bono conjugali*, XXIV, 32.

4. Evagrius *Practical Treatise*, 2.

5. John Cassian *Cenobitic Institutions*, VI, 6.

6. See G. Sfameni Gasparro *Enkrateia e antropologia. Le motivazioni protologiche della continenza e della virginita nel cristianesimo dei primi secoli e nello gnosticismo* (*Studia Ephemeridis Augustinianum*, 20) (Rome 1984).

7. '... in Catholicism power always progresses under the guise of the sacred; that is, more or less under the guise of a prohibition', H. Chaigne, in *Pouvoirs*, No. 17 (1981) 27.

8. R. Gryson 'Dix ans de récherches sur les origines du célibat ecclesiastique', *Revue Théologique de Louvain*, No. 2 (1980) 168, which adds the following: 'When the Eucharist came to be celebrated daily, as happened in the West from the end of the fourth century, it meant lifelong continence for major clergy, whether married or not'.

9. See *Acta apostolicae sedis* (1954), Vol. LXVI, 169–170.

10. The ancient concept of pollution is matter for ethnological studies, which have seen it as a very refined classificatory logic without any moral connotations. Hence the Christian tradition's use of texts from Leviticus changes their meaning considerably.

11. *L'amour du censeur. Essai sur l'ordre dogmatique* (Paris 1974) 69.

12. E. Fuchs *op. cit.* 123ff.

13. J. Lynch 'Critique of the law of celibacy in the Catholic Church from the period of the Reforming Councils', *Concilium* 78 (1972) 53–68.

14. Quoted by Legendre *op. cit.* 127.

15. J. Calvin *Institution de la réligion chrestienne* (1560), IV, XII, 23.

16. *Id.* 24.

17. '... Moses recorded an equality [between man and woman]. Hence we refute the error of those who think that woman was created solely to propagate the human race ... as if she had been given to him [i.e. to man] merely to sleep with him, and not so that she could be his lifelong companion ...', J. Calvin *Commentaires sur la Genèse* (2.18).

Karl Gabriel

Power in the contemporary Church in the light of sociological theories: Max Weber, Michel Foucault and Hannah Arendt

1. POWER IN THE CHURCH AS A GAP IN THE SOCIOLOGY OF RELIGION

THE DISCUSSION of the sociology of the Church that began in the 1930s has omitted the subject of power and its exercise in the Church. The sociology of religion was preoccupied with other problems and other subjects. The foreground was occupied by the question of the changes in participation by members of the Church and the social components of this. The Church itself and in particular its power structures and its processes of the formation of power remained outside the field of view of the sociology of religion. As was brought out by the criticism of this discipline that began in the 1960s this was not the result of accident or a lack of resources. Rather, in its perspectives and basic principles the early sociology of religion was too bound up with the interests of the (official) Church for a sociological look at Church structures to have fitted suitably into its scope. More recent sociology of religion regards ecclesiastical phenomena as so unimportant that getting involved with them does not seem very profitable. Hence until now there has been lacking any lengthy tradition of sociological analysis of the phenomena of ecclesiastical power. A certain exception is provided by the application of Max Weber's concept of power and domination to Church structures, an application which can be traced back to initial attempts in Weber himself. Consequently I would like to start this essay by analysing the phenomena of Church power in the light of Weber's conception and then go on against this background to apply Michel Foucault's and Hannah Arendt's theories of power to the phenomena of Church power and its exercise. The analysis is intended to focus on the level of particular Churches and dioceses.

2. POWER, DOMINATION, DISCIPLINE: MAX WEBER

Max Weber's well-known definition of power ties the phenomenon of power to every opportunity of being able to force one's own will—even against opposition—on the behaviour of others. In the case of religious power the opportunity of prevailing rests ultimately on access to and possession of (scarce) goods that promise salvation and that can be granted or withdrawn.[1] Weber regards power in this sense as too amorphous and frail a phenomenon for it to be able to stand at the centre of human relationships of domination and subordination. Hence his interest is in the first place directed to the question how relationships of power become relationships of domination. As far as Weber is concerned domination as power that has been institutionally stabilised exists if the opportunity exists of orders of almost any kind finding obedience among a definable group of people. Weber regards two factors— legitimation and organisation—as decisive for the transformation of power into domination and its becoming stabilised. Without a belief in legitimacy domination cannot on the one hand gain any 'reliable foundation'.[2] On the other hand domination in its everyday life functions to a considerable extent as organisation or administration. For Weber Churches are religious associations of domination that need their members to believe in their legitimacy and depend on the possession and administration of goods that promise salvation.

Corresponding to his general interests what Weber is particularly concerned with is the analysis of the structures of domination of industrially developed capitalist societies. In this context he analyses the transformation of the structure of domination within the Catholic Church as a process of bureaucratisation and centralisation. The central characteristics of this are seen by Weber as an age-old process of separating or 'expropriating' the individual from the means of religious domination, their concentration at the summit and their allocation from above to below. For Weber this historically unique process of expropriation takes place in the context of the destruction of the Church's feudal structures with their multiplicity of forms of autonomous religious domination, a development which for the first time opened up the way for the concentration of the means of religious domination at the summit. The same applies to the second element of this process: the concentration at the summit of the authority to make decisions and the delegation of these powers from above to below in a system of the domination and subordination of offices. Weber sees the significance of Vatican I in its having brought this process to a definite conclusion with its declaration of the pope's universal episcopate.[3]

The Church's new structure of domination as it spread in Germany from the middle of the nineteenth century onwards gave the bishop a strategically important position. On the one hand he fitted into the centralist and hierarchical organisational structure and was exposed to the continuous supervision of the Roman Curia at the centre. On the other hand he became the master of a diocesan administration that was becoming more sophisticated and of a body of priests who for the first time in the history of the Church found themselves economically in his power. This development created the conditions for the formation and disciplining of the clergy that took place in the second half of the nineteenth century and was carried out by reforming bishops like Ketteler.[4]

At the level of legitimation Weber's analysis of domination indicates two strategies for safeguarding belief in legitimacy in the fundamentally altered conditions of modern societies. In the first place there is the stress on the charismatic person particularly of the pope but also in a derived form of bishops and priests; in the second place there is the strategy of emphasis on tradition in the sense of the conscious cultivation of a traditional popular piety and of the organisation of mass religiosity.

3. THE EXERCISE OF POWER AS THE INCULCATION OF DISCIPLINE: MICHEL FOUCAULT

Michel Foucault shares with Max Weber an interest in the analysis of specific modern structures and techniques of power. The two are linked by the idea that power and domination take on in the modern world the form of the inculcation of various disciplines and that modern societies can therefore with complete justification be characterised as societies based on discipline. Foucault however avoids the problem of the institutionalisation of power that stood at the centre of Weber's concerns. In its place we have the detailed historical analysis of the development of modern techniques of power and of the relationship between knowledge and power.

For Foucault battle provides the paradigm of social relationships, and social behaviour always bears the character of strategic activity.[5] Power as the ability to prevail in strategic activity is seen by Foucault as the central element of every social system. What appears as social order is in reality a momentary result of the continual battle and application of power. In this battle those on the one side do not 'possess' all the power, just as the others are never completely powerless. Foucault regards as mistaken an analytical perspective that sees the phenomenon of power localised exclusively in the apparatus of the State. Power is a phenomenon that lies deeper than that, and State power functions only as the 'instrument of a system of powers that extend far beyond it ...'[6] Foucault regards as equally mistaken the assumption that power is an instrument of the mode of production that happens to prevail at the time. As Foucault has tried to prove specifically with regard to the capitalist mode of production, it was modern power and discipline with their subordination of time to the time of production that first made possible the capitalist mode of production. The productive function of power is also emphasised by Foucault in relationship to knowledge. If one considered power only in its function of suppression one would not become aware of its true potential. Foucault regards power as strong if and only if it does not impede but rather encourages knowledge.

At the core of Foucault's theory of power is the question of which techniques of gaining and exercising power are used by modern highly developed societies for their integration. For him it is beyond doubt that neither the use of force on the one hand nor on the other shared values, internalised norms or ideological indoctrination provide a sufficient measure of affecting behaviour. Foucault centres his analysis of modern techniques of power around the concepts norm, body and knowledge. Modern kinds of techniques of power are characterised by a productive channelling of abilities in the sense of activity being disciplined and turned into a routine so that it becomes a firm habit declared to be 'normal'. In the place of moral norms of activity there appears the norm as compulsive social normality and current social reality. The primary locus of the modern exercise of power is not for Foucault cultural patterns of thought but physical bodies and their expressions of life. As 'microphysics' modern techniques of power are directed towards controlling and disciplining the way in which the body moves in order to train the individual's movements and gestures so that they become productive activities that are automatically on call. The second pole these techniques of power possess alongside disciplining the body is the direction of the population's biological behaviour: the control of reproduction, of birth and death rates and of the level of health of the population.

For Foucault the modern techniques of power develop their full effectiveness through combining with knowledge to form a circle of regulation. Techniques of the exercise of power obtain their rules from the scientific deduction of the corresponding physical and biological processes. The other way round, it is only within the framework of modern systems of power like the clinic or the prison that one reaches an 'epistemological loss of inhibition' and a new form of the accumulation of knowledge. Power produces knowledge, just as the other way round for Foucault there is no knowledge that does not at the same time presuppose relationships of power. Foucault regards social institutions like the clinic, the prison, the factory and the school, as well as the corresponding scientific and professional discourse, as the agents of the exercise of power and the primary locus for the transformation of knowledge into power and *vice versa*.

What insights can be gained from Foucault's theory of power for the exercise of power in the contemporary Church, even if one does not share absolutely Foucault's sociological premises and all aspects of his theory of power?[7] In his historical analyses Foucault himself continually refers to the religious and ecclesiastical origins of the modern techniques of power. But for Foucault they achieved their breakthrough only at the moment when they burst the religious and ecclesiastical framework and made themselves independent and radical in their own logic. In Foucault's perspective the modern techniques of power can be interpreted precisely as an answer to the disintegration of the Church-controlled medieval structure of power and the demands of power that arise from the conditions of integration of modern societies.

But from Weber's analysis of domination we know that in its struggle for existence during the nineteenth century the Catholic Church modernised its structure of domination by reaching back to its own tradition and to a certain extent brought it up to date. If one follows this idea, the question arises of how many of the modern techniques of power brought to light by Foucault have gained entry in one form or another into the exercise of power in the Church. To put it another way, with the help of Foucault's technique of analysis, can more light be shed on the process of inculcating discipline that established itself within the Church during the nineteenth century? In this context no more than a first cautious examination of this question is possible.

The first thing to come within the scope of an analysis of this kind is the Tridentine seminary, which in the nineteenth century became the instrument in the bishop's hand for reforming the training of priests. As is shown by the example of Bishop Ketteler, the bishops now made it their duty to breathe into their seminary 'the spirit of living devotion through the means of spiritual oversight, direction and practice ...'[8] The seminary became the place of a 'body of priests modelled on the same pattern year after year'.[9] A central role in this was played by the practice of a disciplined style of life and of habits that could be reproduced at any time. With the introduction of the minor seminary the channelling of abilities and the formation of standard-setting habits began as early as childhood. Foucault's perspective directs attention in this to the role of hitherto little considered techniques of physical discipline. By way of monastic discipline the techniques for the control and discipline of the body that were perfected in the total institutions of the nineteenth century found their way into seminary discipline. The influence of the idea of total educational social control found expression even in the architecture of seminaries. The important role for discipline within the Church of the law of celibacy, which in the nineteenth century was being freshly insisted on and which in practice prevailed, finds an illuminating explanation within Foucault's frame of reference. For Foucault control over sexuality belongs to the most important techniques of power relating to the body.

The third pole of Foucault's theory of power—the close link between knowledge and power—also reveals new and interesting directions for our questions. The rapidly expanding diocesan administrations became not merely places where power was exercised but also at the same time places where knowledge was formed. At the centre of the new relationships of power and knowledge there stood the institutionalisation and systematisation of the way in which information is diffused within the Church. The questions in this area extend as far as the role of Church statistics and the function of increasing application to the Church, from the 1930s on, of the sociology of religion. In this an important role was from the start played by the experience and the consciousness of a loss of power and control on the part of the Church and the question of effective counter-strategies. If Foucault's theory of power is allowed to lead to a systematic analysis, then finally questions have to be asked about the functional imperatives that led to the new techniques of power being adopted or fashioned in the Church. The process of inculcating discipline that established itself in the nineteenth century and has marked the Church up to the present can be interpreted as a defensive reaction to the new contemporary situation it found itself in with regard to the State and society. It was with a disciplined, blindly co-ordinated social body inured to discipline that the Church of the nineteenth century faced what was perhaps the greatest challenge of its history. In this struggle it fell back, too, on those modern techniques of power which in Foucault's perspective represent the necessary obverse of the bourgeois freedoms of the Enlightenment.

4. POWER AS AUTHORISATION: HANNAH ARENDT

Up to the present day the sociological discussion of power has been marked by different or opposing traditions. Weber and Foucault are to be ascribed to that dominant tradition which sees the core of the phenomenon of power in making one's own will prevail even against opposition. In contrast to this is a tradition which reaches back to the ancient world and which sees power as linked to agreement and authorisation by the members of a social association. Hannah Arendt consciously falls back on this tradition of thought when she criticises as inadequate the model of power oriented towards giving orders and obedience. 'Power,' she writes, 'corresponds to the human ability not just to act but to act in concert.'[10] Hence one is mistaken if with Max Weber and many others one sees in force or violence the culmination of power. For Hannah Arendt violence is something which an individual with the right means can inflict on many others, but in contrast 'power is never the property of an individual; it belongs to a group and remains in existence only so long as the group keeps together'.[11] Violence may compel obedience but it does not provide the foundation for power. The origin of power lies for Hannah Arendt in the decision to act jointly and together: corresponding to this the claim to power is legitimate by appeal to the past. It is also of interest in the context of our present discusison to see how Hannah Arendt understands 'authority'. She sees the decisive hallmark of authority in 'unquestioning recognition by those who are asked to obey'.[12] The foundation of authority is respect for the person or office possessing authority: everything that undermines this is dangerous for authority. In contrast to power, authority 'can be vested in persons ... or it can be vested in offices'.[13] As a typical form of authority vested in an office Hannah Arendt indicates the hierarchical offices of the Church with the *ex opere operato* understanding of the sacraments.

What questions and insights can be gained from Hannah Arendt's theory of power for the problem of the exercise of power in the Church? The first thing that emerges from her perspective is that a Church freed of power would entail as a pre-condition the dissolution of the Church as a social group. As long as the Church exists as a group of people acting together power is formed within it. This applies at the level of the universal Church, of the diocese, of the parish community, as well as at the level of a group within the parish community. But at all levels power in its actual social existence is linked to the assent of the members of the group. Thus bishops as formal bearers of the position of power in the diocese only possess power to the extent that they meet with assent among the people of God. Even the question of the specific form the power-structure takes retreats to second place behind the necessity of support from the people making up the Church. Thus an episcopate structured on monarchical lines needs not less but more support from the people than a democratic one in order to be able in practice to exercise power.

If one follows Hannah Arendt's theory of power, a precarious situation emerges for the exercise of power in and by the Church in the contemporary world. Both pope and bishops are faced with the problem of gaining acceptance and thus in practice obtaining power without being able to fall back on formal means of authorisation from below. In view of the multiplication of different lifestyles and different patterns of interpretation among Catholics too, it becomes ever more difficult for those who formally have power to obtain a broad measure of agreement and support. It should not therefore be surprising that there has been an overt loss of power with regard to 'conservative' groups on the one hand and 'progressive' ones on the other. What becomes clear here is that the loss of power is linked to symptoms of partial dissolution of the Church as a social group. Even greater significance attaches to a second phenomenon which is rather hard to comprehend: the emergence of a certain power vacuum within the Church. The withdrawal of assent is not matched by any new formation of power. The silent retreat of Church members from the Church as a social group belongs to this context. Further references can be established within the pattern of interpretation suggested by Hannah Arendt's theory of power. The modern Church is denied the typical reaction to loss of power—having recourse to force. The Church's interest in its members' 'obedience' consequently must concentrate completely on 'authority as unquestioning recognition' of its claim to obedience. Hannah Arendt sees the basis of 'the severest crisis of the Church as an institution' to lie precisely in the fact that it has to rely on its authority alone at a time when 'the atom "obedience" whose stability was allegedly eternal' is threatened with being progressively exploded.[14] One could perhaps add that emphasis on claims to authority in the face of loss of power contributes precisely to the exacerbation of the problem. In Hannah Arendt's perspective the necessary relief could be obtained by authority in the Church through the development of new forms of the recognition of power by the people of God. The ecclesiology of Vatican II has opened up possibilities of taking the power of the many in the Church more seriously than hitherto. In realising these possibilities, what is at stake—both empirically and theoretically—is the integration of the Church as a social group.

5. DISCIPLINE INSTEAD OF AUTHORISATION?

It is not easy to sum up all these observations. The differences between the distinctive theories of power cited here seem to be too great for an agreed picture to become recognisable. But some cautious conclusions can all the same be drawn. Following Max Weber it became clear that, despite its emphatically 'antimodernist' orientation and sharp delimitation from the external world, the Catholic Church in the nineteenth century underwent a modernisation of its structure of domination comparable to that experienced by the other social institutions. The development that established itself in the nineteenth century has in principle continued to set its stamp on the Church up to the present. Even Vatican II made little change to the concentration of jurisdiction and powers at the summit of the universal Church and of the diocese.[15] With reference to Foucault's theory of power it is merely the dimensions that are of primary interest that shift, while in the total perspective at least partial agreements can be recognised. The importance of discipline for the modern form of domination is already established with Max Weber. Foucault radicalises this perspective and resolves domination in need of legitimation into techniques of the exercise of power that cloak themselves in a humanitarian phraseology. Here too it became clear that Foucault's viewpoint made more things recognisable with regard to modern techniques of power in the Church than might have been expected from an institution that is generally classified as notoriously 'antiquated'. With her concept of power Hannah Arendt clings to an option that Max Weber and especially Foucault had long since given up: of its nature power is linked to authorisation by the social group concerned. The comparison makes it clear that the choice of one's conceptual and theoretical starting-point already involves in advance wide-ranging decision of what can come under scrutiny. For Weber and Foucault, modern relations of domination and subordination are not or are no longer to be understood on the basis of the problem of joint action, whereas Hannah Arendt seeks to deduce social reality from forms of popular power. In this sense one could try to link the two perspectives together. What would apply to the Church as to the rest of society would then be that, where recognition and support are lacking, techniques of power in Foucault's sense gain ground.

Translated by Robert Nowell

Notes

1. Max Weber *Wirtschaft und Gesellschaft*, ed. J. Winckelmann (Cologne/Berlin 1964) pp. 38ff., 157ff., 691ff.
2. Max Weber op. cit. p. 157.
3. Max Weber op. cit. p. 1047.
4. Cf. Michael N. Ebertz 'Herrschaft in der Kirche. Hierarchie, Tradition und Charisma im 19. Jahrhundert', in K. Gabriel and F. X. Kaufmann (ed.) *Zur Soziologie des Katholizismus* (Mainz 1980) pp. 96ff.
5. On this and what follows see primarily 'Le Pouvoir et la norme' in Delenze and Foucault *Pouvoir et surface* (no date, no place of publication) reprinted in Foucault *Mikrophysik der Macht* (Berlin 1976) pp. 99–107; Foucault *Surveillir et punir* (Paris 1975); Foucault *Naissance de la Clinique* (Paris 1972).

6. Michel Foucault *Mikrophysik der Macht*, p. 100.

7. For criticism along these lines see Axel Honneth *Kritik der Macht. Reflexionsstufen einer kritischen Gesellschaftstheorie* (Frankfurt 1985) pp. 113–224.

8. F. Vigener *Ketteler. Ein deutscher Bischof des 19. Jahrhunderts* (Munich/Berlin 1924) quoted here from Ebertz, art. cit. (note 4), p. 99.

9. Vigener *Ketteler*, p. 289.

10. Hannah Arendt *On Violence* (London 1970) p. 44.

11. Arendt op. cit. p. 44.

12. Arendt op. cit. p. 45.

13. Arendt op. cit. p. 45.

14. Thus Hannah Arendt, quoting a phrase of Heinrich Böll's, op. cit. p. 46 n. 67.

15. See A. Acerbi 'Die ekklesiologischen Grundlagen der nachkonziliaren Institutionen', in G. Alberigo, Y. Congar and H. J. Pottmeyer (ed.) *Kirche im Wandel. Eine kritische Zwischenbilanz nach dem Zweiten Vatikanum* (Düsseldorf 1982) pp. 208–240.

Wigand Siebel

The Exercise of Power in Today's Church

1. POWER AND RULE

POWER AS the actually existing pre-eminence of one person over another is an inherent characteristic of all social relationships. Every way of exercising an influence over other people means power, whether this influence be personal, or whether it be exercised by way of some particular instrument over which the person disposes. The instrument may be a winning personality, a woman's erotic attraction, the money in someone's pocket, or the revolver in his hand. Power is already part of the relationship between two people, so that one of them is subject to the power of the other. And yet no one is completely without power unless he is unconscious in the medical sense (for which the German word, significantly, is *ohnmächtig*—powerless). This means that all power is confronted with counter-power, even in the tiniest group. And in this light, social relationships are always sustained by a power structure, and are aligned towards a balance of power.

Power may be exercised for a wide variety of purposes. The purpose can be some advantage for the person exercising the power (for example, the acquisition of profit); it may be the welfare of those subject to that power (for example, in education or upbringing); or it may be the benefit of a third person or group. In this third category, the social systems on whose behalf power can be exercised are particularly important. Social systems, whether they be families, associations or clubs, parties or countries, generally possess an accumulated power that is not affected by death in the physical sense. So here

39

the question about the misuse of power confronts us in a particular way. If all power comes up against a counter-power, then it is all the more essential for the exercise of great, far-reaching and dangerous power to be subjected to some counter-power; and this means controls.

Whatever may be the individual methods of controlling power, those who exercise power in all social systems are subject to processes of control which have to take their bearings from legitimating norms. Legitimate power is socially accepted power, power which feels bound to the objectives, standards and traditions of the social system and tries to act in a way that will be in line with the maintenance and welfare of the whole. Seen in this way, legitimate power may be called rule. When power is exercised through acts of rule, these acts represent the social system and its members. We might say that the social system is able to act itself by way of the people who are its rulers. Thus, by way of its representatives, the social system establishes partial internal norms, imposing punishments when these norms are flouted; while outwardly it acts by being able to bind all its members, both in the present and for the future (for example—in the case of a country—by concluding international agreements).

Recent philosophical theories about the problems of power have particularly stressed the way in which power is woven into social relationships. To take an example: Hannah Arendt (1906–1975) made a name for herself by stressing the positive aspects of power. She tells us, for instance, that 'Power preserves the public realm and the space of appearance, and as such it is also the lifeblood of the human artifice'.[1] Here power is understood, not merely as potentiality, but as relationship—as something that binds people together. 'Power is never the property of an individual; it belongs to a group and remains in existence only so long as the group keeps together.'[2] The mutual relationship of power permits the realisation of freedom, in which communication can develop through the processes of argument and conviction. Tyranny is the vain attempt to replace power through force.[3]

Michel Foucault (1926–1984) stressed a similar idea: 'Power is not an institution and not a structure. Nor is it the power of a single powerful person. Power is the name we give to a complex strategic situation in a given society.'[4] 'Power is not possessed. It works ... on the whole surface of the social field according to a system of relays, connections, transmissions, distributions, etc. Power works through the smallest elements: the family, social relationships, but also living conditions, neighbours, etc. However far we go in the social network, we always discover power as something that 'runs through it all', something that has an effect, that effectuates.'[5] The question that concerns Foucault here is: 'In western societies, how is the production of discourses which are charged with a truth value (at least for a certain time) bound to the different power mechanisms and institutions?'[6]

In his book *Surveiller et punir* (ET *Discipline and Punishment*) Foucault has developed a picture of society as a 'prison city', whose model is the gaol, as panoptic system of surveillance and discipline. From this viewpoint, everything which appears to us to be a humanised working world or penal system or school or hospital is a 'global mechanism for silently gathering in the masses for the purpose of training them effectively in a particular direction'.[7] While trying to dissociate himself from certain Marxist conceptions, Foucault maintains no systematic theory of power. He suggests that his readers should use his books as 'boxes of tools', in order at need to set up new discourses with these conceptions, and so as to illuminate and 'take apart' the systems of power inherent in them.[8] He therefore continually asks under what foretokens systems of power stand; for it is essential—and particularly for the sociologist—to analyse these systems critically.

2. THE LEGITIMATION OF ECCLESIASTICAL POWER

(a) The Spheres of Legitimation

In all social systems power finds its legitimation on three different levels: there is the legitimation of the office, the legitimation of the person, and the legitimation of the acts of rule that are actually carried out. The first form of legitimation—*the legitimation of the office*—asks about the sphere of responsibility and its justification in the framework of the whole social system, with its tradition. The second form of legitimation—*the legitimation of the person*—asks whether the office has been properly assumed by the person holding it (e.g., whether the choice or election was valid). The third form of legitimation, finally—*the legitimation of particular actions*—asks whether what the ruling person does is in accordance with law (in the wider sense of justice, not merely in the sense of a definite law in force). The legitimation of action can be defined least readily. But it presupposes that a ruling person who is in another sense legitimated can still lose that legitimation through an unlawful act of rule. When unlawful acts by rulers are controlled by members of the social system, this ensures that the legitimation process is fundamentally speaking never at an end.

Where the Church is concerned, its offices have received their legitimation through the divine institution of the Church and its most important ministries. Added to this is the reference to tradition, which has always known these ministries. The legitimation of a particular person, as entitled to fulfil a particular function in the Church, presents no essential problems. But the legitimation of acts of rule—which is to say the exercise of ecclesiastical power—requires more detailed discussion; and we shall turn to that now.

(b) Possible Means of Legitimation

For the legislation of its acts of rule also, the Church can and will appeal to its divine commission. But this 'formal' aspect or viewpoint does not take us far enough. There must also be substantial criteria, which can be objectively tested. If we compare today's Church with the Church that existed previously, we can discover two different substantial principles according to which the Church mainly acted (or still acts), and through which it justifies itself and its exercise of power. The one principle is the conservation and dissemination of the *depositum fidei*, the faith entrusted to it; the other may be called the duty to preserve unity.

The principle of the conservation and dissemination of the depositum fidei belongs mainly to the earlier Church. The *depositum fidei*, as the faith passed on to the Church by Christ and the apostles, had to be safeguarded, defended against all attack, and interpreted so as to save souls from the world, which was under the power of Satan. For only belief in this depository of faith—that is to say, in the divine revelation—was considered to be salvific. The Church saw itself as the agency of God's message to men and women, offering them salvation in faith through its goodly message, the gospel.

The principle that the Church is in duty bound to promote unity is held primarily in the Church of today. It demands that ecclesiastical rule—and ultimately every Christian—must be directed towards unity, and must deliberately move towards the attainment of this goal. In this light, history appears as a trend towards unity, which is fundamentally to be attained as the unity of Christians and the unity of all.

The one principal can be interpreted more or elss statically. The other principle is dynamic. Of course the two principles can never be found in chemically pure form, either in the past or the present. In considering today's Church we shall proceed only from the predominance of the second principle.

3. LEGITIMATION THROUGH UNITY

(a) Conceptions of Unity

Unity is not in itself a completely unequivocal goal. It has various stages and may be realised in many different ways, all of which have to be considered in the light of the ultimate goal. In order to make this clear let us consider a statement made by Cardinal Ratzinger: 'I am convinced that the question of when all Christians will be united is in fact unanswerable. For we must not forget that the question about the unity of Israel and the Church also belongs here ... The complete unity of all Christians will hardly be attainable in this era. But the unity of the one Church which already indestructibly exists is for us the guarantor that this greater unity will sometime or other come. The more we strive towards this unity with all our powers, the more Christian we are.'[9] According to this statement, there is the unity of the one Church; and this already exists. There is also the unity of all Christians. Finally, a unity between Israel and the Church still has to be brought about. Since the unity that already exists cannot be the unity of the Catholic church (since that would sound like ecumenism by way of a 'return to the fold'), what must be meant here is the idea of the Church founded by Jesus Christ, which is embodied in all the churches that actually exist.

But the unity of Israel and the Church cannot be the final unity. Bishop Klaus Hemmerle, for example, writes: 'Humanity is on the search for the true unity: ultimately this is the keynote of the age in which we live. The one word that touches the heart of our era is the word unity ... The one question—but also the deepest one—is: why is *unity* particularly the key word in God's history with men and women? Why does God desire, not only the unity of every individual with him, but also the unity of all human beings with one another? The answer is himself, it is the innermost mystery of God himself.'[10] So what is in question is unity *per se*—a limitless unity which no longer draws a dividing line against those outside. This idea of unity is essentially co-formative of the stages in which the unity comes into being.

If it is this unity towards which the Church is aligned, then the Church itself takes on the character of an instrument on the path towards this all-comprehensive unity. This is in fact the way Vatican II saw the Church. The Church, it said, is 'the sign and instrument ... for the unity of all humanity' (*Lumen gentium* 1). According to this, the Church sees itself as a sacrament which both signifies and effects the unity of all.

(b) The Ambivalence of Rule

Normally, rule is exercised from a single standpoint, that of the social system which it represents. But in today's Church, rule has to assume at least two positions, either simultaneously or alternately: on the one hand the position of the Church as it has come down to us; on the other hand, the standpoint of unity. In fact, however, ecclesiastical power is not merely exercised from two standpoints. The positions are really several, being derived from the various stages the unity has reached. Accordingly, the concept of the Church itself also has various stages or domains. This being so, ecclesiastical rule is compelled to represent several unities, either simultaneously or successively. This means that the people subject to the Church's rule always have to ask from which standpoint the representative of that rule is speaking in any given case. Is he starting from *de facto* unity, from Christian unity, from the unity of the Abrahamic religions, from the unity of all religions, or from the unity of all human beings? For different conclusions will have to be drawn according to the answer given.

From this point of view, the Church's rule is no longer identifiable in a clear-cut way. The norms that were hitherto valid have lost the clarity of their application. Rule in general seems ambivalent and no longer tangible. Consequently the binding power of the Church's sway is bound to diminish and the identification of believers with the Church is bound to recede. This is confirmed by empirical investigations. Largely speaking, men and women no longer feel obliged to follow the directives of the ecclesiastical power. At the same time, when the authorities in the Church act officially, they are increasingly ceasing to be seen *as* authorities. They appear rather as advisers or friends—and this is what they themselves claim to be. This can be welcomed as for all practical purposes a gradual demolition of structures of rule.

(c) The Priority of Praxis

If the exercise of power is legitimated largely by the principle that it is an obligation to promote unity, then the given accompaniment will be a praxis which all Christians have to follow. As we saw, Cardinal Ratzinger also said that 'the more we move towards this unity with all our powers, the more Christian we are'. So it is no longer essentially a matter of the truth of certain doctrinal positions. The essential point is progress towards unity, although here the true unity also seems to embrace the truth.

It would seem obvious to take this praxis into the political sector, for even though the unity of all is a Utopia, it is none the less a political idea which requires political action. It is true that the action is not necessarily politics in the traditional sense; but it is nevertheless a kind of politics, which must therefore be drawn into the exercise of the Church's power. Clodovis Boff writes, for example: 'A new ethic of struggle is taking shape alongside and as part of the new concept of politics among the poor of Latin America. By "ethic" I understand the way an action is carried out, a way of acting, a basic mode of behaviour. For the sake of simplifying, this term can be taken to include *what comes before action, a mystique,* and *what comes after, a strategy.*'[11]

What precedes praxis is assigned to the praxis itself. This has parallels in Marxism. But here it is not the 'theory' that succeeds the praxis but the 'mysticism'. It is true that the idea of unity has a mystical component, simply because it is utopian, but also because it is capable of evoking 'ecumenical enthusiasm' (Ratzinger's phrase).

4. STRUCTURES OF POWER AS IT IS EXERCISED WITHIN THE CHURCH ITSELF

(a) Guidance through the Utopia?

The idea of unity is a Utopia inasmuch as this unity does not in actual fact exist. It is a certain condition which is proclaimed as a future and desirable form of organisation for human beings—one which will bring happiness for all. And since this is a desirable goal, it exercises an attraction.

This condition will be at least a state of peace, righteousness and love. That can be deduced from the various statements made by Paul VI, and especially by John Paul II when, talking about 'the civilisation of love', he says that it is a goal 'towards which all our efforts in the social, cultural, economic and political sectors must be directed'.[12] And in 1985 the Extraordinary Synod of Bishops said similarly: 'There is a way for humanity, and we are already seeing the first signs of it—a way that leads forward to a civilisation of partnership, solidarity and love, a civilisation which is alone worthy of men and women.'[13]

This idea is supposed to fire us all. God's people is thought of as being on the way towards this Utopia. That is why—among all the images used to describe the Church—the image of the 'pilgriming' messianic people of God has come to take precedence in the proclamation. In the light of this goal (which is conceived of as attainable), the world now appears as lovable and desirable; for the world makes the union of all possible, and itself finds expression in this objective. In earlier days, the Church wished to set itself firmly apart from the world. In the eyes of today's Church, in contrast, the position of the world has been positively reversed.

The world, then, as the union of all in the civilisation of love represents a condition of perfection. But in this case the world must contain a kind of holiness, a holiness in which all human beings already participate. This being so, it would seem impossible for anyone to be lost. If God desires unity, then in his plan of salvation he must also have foreseen the salvation of everyone. Consequently judgment appears in countless variations as meaningless, and hell as empty. This idea is most consistently pursued in the postulate that all human beings have become God's children through the incarnation of Christ, and with sanctifying grace have received the Holy Spirit.[14]

(b) The Increased Requirement for Legitimation

The alignment towards unity does not merely provide the ecclesiastical power with a criterion whereby to legitimate its actions, however. This criterion must also be presented in itself as meaningful and convincing: the ways to unity must be discovered, investigated and publicly explored. If it were impossible to show that unity is a credible goal, then this very fact would call in question the legitimation of the acts involved—indeed the legitimation of the persons concerned could suffer.

This means that, where the power of the Church is concerned, the need for legitimation has increased enormously. The power of the Church in its official capacity cannot possibly satisfy this need all by itself. Consequently, in a tremendous turn-about, the theologians have been assigned the task of legitimating the Church's actions. What theology was in the past, it has now ceased to be (except for a few sectors, such as church history). As example we may point to the complete cessation of controversial theology. Theology has come to see itself essentially as ecumenical theology—that is to say, a theology which has to further unity in a series of practical steps. By furthering this aim, it also offers far-reaching assistance to the Church's structure of power, legitimating it in the light of the goal, and suggesting the paths of progress leading to that goal. It is true that tensions arise here too, when the official Church does not always assent to the ways proposed, or if its assent is not sufficiently complete.[15] But the mutual dependence of the official church and the theologians none the less remains.

In actual fact this means a considerable expansion of the power of the theologians in the Church. One example is the periodical *Concilium*, which is able to appear in seven languages. All in all, we find that the official Church and theology (as the centre from which the Church exercises its power) share a relatively stable power structure, in which the two are dovetailed in a way that has never hitherto existed in the Church's history. Each side is checked and balanced by the other, and is prompted to particular actions. And here it is by no means the case that the official Church always has the upper hand. Occasional disciplinary action against theologians who call in question the power of the official Church has not been able to impair this fundamental co-operation in the exercise of the Church's power.

(c) Means of Communicating with the World

Ever since Vatican II, dialogue has been stressed as the central medium for bringing about unity and for communicating with the world. This dialogue must not be conceived as a discourse free of all control. On the contrary, the dialogue is carried on fundamentally in the name of the ecclesiastical power—in the context of ecumenical discussion, in the name of the authorities of the churches concerned, and on their instructions. Here both themes and objectives are laid down authoritatively in advance. The point at issue is mutual understanding, and hence the awakening and fortifying of the readiness for commitment on behalf of unity. It is also a matter, quite explicitly, of the practical advance towards the goal of unity. It is the theologians who are involved in the dialogue first of all—or it may be officials of the Church who can also be viewed as theologians.

Another way of building a bridge to the world, however, is the *liturgy*. Shared practices of devotion in ecumenical services of worship serve to promote unity. But this is also true of the Eucharist, which is increasingly interpreted as a means for strengthening general community and fellowship, and as a way of furthering brotherhood by way of the common meal. The sacrificial view held by the Church earlier (which was isolating) has been abandoned.

5. STRUCTURES OF POWER EXERCISED OUTWARDS

(a) The Incorporation of Forces that Further Unity

Since unity is the desired destination, all the forces that are to be included in this unity must be more firmly incorporated in the Church's structure of power. This is true particularly of the forces which are already demanding unity on their own initiative. This may be said first of all of groups such as the charismatic movement, the Focolare, etc., and then of the ecumenical movement in the Christian churches themselves. Here there must be growing co-operation between the different communions, from the Free churches to the Orthodox. Above all, the World Council of Churches will have increasingly to be drawn into the Roman church's process of arriving at decisions. Rome's assent, largely speaking, to the Lima document has recently strengthened the links between Rome and Geneva.

But non-Christian forces—Judaism, Islam, Freemasonry and Marxism—must also be brought in, when decisions are arrived at. For all these bodies pursue similar goals, at least to some degree. On the one hand this makes actual rule more difficult, because a multiplicity of concerns and viewpoints have to be drawn into the decisions arrived at. On the other hand, commissions and institutions are increasingly creating the readiness and will for co-operation and unity.

(b) The Relationship to the State

According to the principle that directed the actions of the Church earlier, the Christian state was the ideal, and the obligation to obey the state power was generally stressed, following Romans 13. But the principle of unity requires furtherance of the liberal state, which concedes the same rights to all religions and philosophies of life. In this way the state is put under an obligation to co-operate in working for the unity towards which the Church is striving. The principle of religious liberty which Vatican II proclaimed (stating that all religions—and therefore their members too—must be granted the right to practise their religion freely) is thus a necessary pre-condition if the idea of unity is to be decisively advanced in the political sector as well.

On the other hand, governmental rule is always basically under suspicion of misuse. This follows from the mere fact that, because of its specific geographical limits, the state has a certain trend towards particularity. Consequently, if unity is the overriding aim, the state's claim to obedience must be relaxed, especially where possible armed conflict is concerned.

(c) Liberation as a Task

If unity is understood as a limitless unity embracing all and everyone, this means fundamentally liberation from all frontiers and confines. To this extent unity is a Utopia that is intimately connected with liberty. It is therefore not at all surprising that the official Church should have accepted liberation theology as a common Christian concern. Here liberation must be understood as a process that leads away from all the confining conditions of power. Basically, therefore, the road to unity involves a revolutionary element which will resist the static conditions of power.

If the kingdom of peace, which is also the kingdom of unity, is to be attained, it is valuable to engender a critical attitude towards all forms of unjustified domination, and to encourage the will to resist them. Moreover, unity would appear to be a condition lacking forms of domination. Rule can no longer be accepted without examination, and has to justify itself, whether in marriage and the family, society or state. So the Church's attitude to the state will increasingly require that the state too legitimate itself.

(d) The End of the Road

Unity is a Utopia, but a 'real' Utopia. That is to say, it can one day be fulfilled. The world as unity could be brought into being in the fullest sense. Whether peace, justice and love will then really rule must remain an open question. But what is then going to happen to the Church? It will at all events lose its legitimation as 'sign and instrument' of the world's unity. But if the Church once makes itself dispensible, then the long-awaited civilisation of love could, without the Church, turn into a realisation of Foucault's vision of 'the prison city'. It would therefore indeed be well if the end of the road were to coincide with Christ's second coming. But that is not the same thing as the realised Utopia of unity. How is this impasse to be resolved?

Translated by Margaret Kohl

Notes

1. Hannah Arendt *The Human Condition* (New York 1959) p. 204.
2. Hannah Arendt *On Violence* (New York 1970) p. 44.
3. Hannah Arendt *The Human Condition, op. cit.*, p. 203.
4. Michel Foucault *Historie de la sexualité* I: *la Volonté de savoir* (Paris 1976) p. 123.
5. Michel Foucault *Mikrophysik der Macht* (Berlin 1976) p. 99.
6. Michel Foucault *Sexualität und Wahrheit* I, *Der Wille zum Wissen* (Frankfurt 1977) p. 8. This introduction to the German edition of *Histoire de la sexualité* does not appear in the original French edition.
7. Clemens Kammler *Michel Foucault—Eine kritische Analyse seines Werkes* (Bonn 1986) pp. 169f.
8. Foucault *Mikrophysik op. cit.*, p. 45.
9. Joseph Cardinal Ratzinger *Kirche, Ökumene und Politik* (Einsiedeln 1987).
10. Klaus Hemmerle, 'Einheit—die Sehnsucht unserer Zeit', *Schweizerische Katholische Wochenzeitung* 4, September 1987.
11. Clodovis Boff, 'The Poor of Latin America and their new Ways of Liberation' *Concilium* 191 (1987) *Changing Values and Virtues* p. 38.
12. John Paul II, encyclical 'Dives in misercordia' (1980), n. 14, 7.
13. Extraordinary Synod of Bishops, message of 7 December 1985.
14. John Paul II, encyclical 'Dominum et vivificantem' (1986), n. 52, 3.
15. See, for example, the controversy between Karl Rahner and Heinrich Fries on the one hand, and Cardinal Ratzinger on the other. Cf. here Ratzinger, *op. cit.*

PART II

Hervi Rikhof

The Competence of Priests, Prophets and Kings: Ecclesiological Reflections about the Power and Authority of Christian Believers

1. INTRODUCTION

THERE IS always a risk that theological reflections about power and authority, especially if they are brief, will go to one or other of two extremes. They may on the one hand result in a beautiful and idealistic description, rather vaguely recommending unreal relationships rather than throwing light on real relationships. On the other hand, they may equally well lead to a more or less precise description of the state of affairs in which the reader is either so fascinated by the power game or so disappointed by the cynicism of the facts that the question of alternatives and that of correctness are simply not asked.

I hardly dare to claim that the reflections in this article will not go to one or other of these extremes—or even to both at the same time. I shall, however, try to restrict this danger. To restrict the second, I shall limit myself principally to a theological and ecclesiological framework within which power can be discussed. To restrict the first, I shall take that framework from the *Codex Iuris Canonici* and fill it in with a fairly everyday analysis of competence. The most that I can do in this short article is to outline that framework and indicate where and how it is possible and necessary to speak about power and authority.

A choice for the framework used in the *Codex* leads us, however, to ask about the interpretation of Vatican II and especially that contained in the Dogmatic Constitution on the Church, *Lumen Gentium*. This is inevitable, because the revision of the *Codex* formed from the very beginning part of the process of reform in which the Council played a central role and because the *Codex* has to be interpreted and checked in the light of the Council and not vice versa.[1] This means that several comments have to be made to begin with concerning the reception and interpretation of Vatican II and in particular of *Lumen Gentium*.

2. THE RECEPTION AND INTERPRETATON OF VATICAN II

(a) A Third Phase?

It is clear both from recent writings about Vatican II—occasioned among other things by the Special Synod of 1985—and from various commentaries on the *Codex* that this reception and interpretation has been a discussion point. Generally speaking, this reception and interpretation—in other words the explanation, evaluation, continuing effect and rejection of pronouncements made by a council—form part of that council, as the whole process constitutes the concrete truth of that council. It is only in that whole process, in which the *consensus fidelium* is activated, that the truth of a council is brought to light. And that process is a continuing one, because tradition and the formation of tradition are continuing. In constantly changing circumstances, the past history of faith is discussed as an element in the common search for truth.

Important events in the history of politics and art are often subjected to a changing evaluation. A positive period of enthusiasm is usually followed by a negative period of disappointment and then by a period of synthesis, in which a more balanced appreciation is achieved. That is the model that is also applied to the twenty years since the end of Vatican II. The final period of synthesis is, however, not yet present in this option, although there is a wish for it and there are perceptible signs of it.[2]

However self-evident this model may be and however applicable to the (psychological and sociological) tendencies of our present post-conciliar period, it does not, in my opinion, get to the heart of the problems concerning the reception and interpretation of Vatican II and especially of *Lumen Gentium*. The heart of these problems is to be found in the ambivalence of the text, in other words, of the juxtaposition of two fundamentally different views of the Church and of faith.

This has led to an important complication, because, in addition to the ordinary positive and negative reactions and the inevitable swinging between the two there is also in the whole post-conciliar process a datum of a different kind. That is the ambivalence of the text to which I have alluded above, and the possibility that both sides may appeal to the same text in defence of their different positions. This appeal does not, moreover, either necessarily or in fact coincide with the successive positive and negative phases.

Whenever this complication is not sufficiently borne in mind, the solution of this ambivalence is found in a third synthetic and intermediate phase, in which the one-sided aspects of the preceding phases are overcome within a larger all-embracing framework. On the other hand, whenever it is borne in mind, the problem is viewed differently and the question is asked: Can two fundamentally different views really be combined with each other? The central problem in the reception and interpretation of Vatican II and *Lumen Gentium* then becomes the choice and elaboration through argument of one of these two frameworks, in which elements of the other view may also possibly begin to play a part.

(b) The Choices in *Lumen Gentium*

The text plays a central part in the choice of such a framework. The genesis and the history of the effectiveness of the text may throw further light on its meaning. This may happen because the intentions and the motives of the authors of the text are implicated in its genesis and the intended or unintended possibilities of the text are implied in the history of its effectiveness.

I will not repeat in detail the analyses of the text of *Lumen Gentium* and the history of its development, but will simply say this. The ecclesiological framework is from the very beginning outlined theologically and in terms of the history of salvation in the text. The Church is placed within the framework of God's history with men, a history that extends from the time of creation to the end of time. The Church is also defined as 'a people made one with the unity of the Father, the Son and the Holy Spirit' (*Lumen Gentium* 4). And, as indicated in this definition—'a people made one'—the Church is also understood in this context primarily as the community of all believers. The communal element is of primary importance. The distinguishing element is of secondary importance and it serves the communal element.

It is clear from the genesis of the text, then, that these two elements are the positive expression of the fundamental criticism of triumphalism, clericalism and jurisdicism that was made of the first draft. This criticism in any case reflects both what the bishops did not want and their intention. As such, this criticism is one of the keys to the interpretation of the final text. It is also clear from the genesis of the text that what the bishops really wanted emerged only very gradually and that important conclusions were precisely for this reason not always drawn.[3]

All this can be seen in a very different light in the history of the text's effectiveness, because the imprecision of the terminology, the formal nature of certain compromises—and above all the failure to integrate the text and its inconsistency—have always given rise to different and even mutually contradictory interpretations of *Lumen Gentium*, in which the two elements mentioned above play a central part.

One is bound to conclude from the text itself and the history of its development that the view of the Church that was chosen is a theological one in which the communal element is of primary importance. One is also bound to conclude from the history of the text's effectiveness that these choices were not subjected to consistent thought. In this sense, then, it is possible to describe *Lumen Gentium* as a 'transitory' text.

(c) The *Codex*

Different opinions have been expressed about the reception and interpretation of Vatican II in the *Codex*.[4] If it can be stated that the Council's view of the Church is generally speaking included in the *Codex*, then it has to be added at once that the ambivalence is also included. In addition to a theological view based on the Church as a *communio*, there is also in the *Codex* a socio-philosophical and juridical view based on the Church as a *societas perfecta*, both as far as the foundation of law on the theory of knowledge is concerned and as far as the effect on parts is concerned. It is because of this that the *Codex* is also regarded as a 'transitory solution'.[5]

(d) Conclusions

On the basis of what I have said above, I am bound to affirm that *Lumen Gentium* provides the framework and the necessary points of departure for any theological reflection about power and authority in the Church and that these have also been adopted in the *Codex*. At the same time, I must also say that a further and consistent full consideration in the direction of the choices made and of what is 'fundamentally new'[6] is required for such a theological reflection.

Because of the points of departure provided by *Lumen Gentium*, it is obvious that a reflection about power and authority should not begin with the ministry of the hierarchical authority, but by seeing whether this theme cannot and should not be discussed before—in other words—at the level of what is common to all. That is why two steps have to be taken at this point. The first is to define more precisely what that common element is. The second is to analyse the authority that is applicable to that level.

3. THE SCHEMA OF THE THREE TASKS

(a) Lumen Gentium and the Codex

One of the new aspects in *Lumen Gentium* is not only that the common element is given a position of primary importance, but also that it is expressed with the help of the schema: 'priest-prophet-king'. It is characteristic of what I have called above the 'transitory' nature of *Lumen Gentium* that, on the one hand, this new schema gives a fundamental structure to our thinking about Christian believers and, on the other hand, that its application is problematical. By this I mean that it is not consistently applied—the part dealing with 'king', for example, is absent from Chapter 2 of the Constitution, which deals with the People of God. There are also duplications which are at the same time not duplications, because, for example, every baptised person is sometimes included among the baptised and at other times only lay people are included (see *Lumen Gentium* 10, cf. 31). Other examples of such duplications are the discussion of the hierarchy's ministry in similar terms (*ibid.* 24, cf. 25–27) and the discussion of the universal and hierarchical priesthood (*ibid.* 10).

The *Codex* also makes use of this scheme in its structure and content. Compared with the previous *Codex*, this is a completely new datum. It is used in the structure of the *Codex* in that the titles of certain books (III and IV) point to the three tasks. It appears in its content, among other things, in that the threefold task is included in the definition of the term 'Christian believer' in the first canon of the book dealing with the People of God. But the transitory nature to which I have alluded above is also visible in the *Codex* in this point. The schema is not preserved in the structure of the *Codex*—there is no book, for example, on the royal task—nor are all possible conclusions drawn in its content—for example, in the question of the universal priesthood of all believers and the *sensus fidelium*.[7]

(b) Different Uses

It is clear from an investigation carried out by L. Schick into the origin and use of this scheme that it has been used in the course of history for different purposes and in different contexts.[8] It has, for example, been used Christologically in order to explain the name 'Christ'. This use occurred in the patristic period and the Middle Ages and can be found in the *Catechismus Romanus* of the Council of Trent. It was also used in the context of the doctrine of redemption to express the functions of Christ (see Calvin).

It was also employed—again in the patristic period and the middle ages, but also in the liturgies of both the Western and the Eastern Churches—in theological anthropology to indicate the dignity and the rights and duties of every Christian. It is also to be found from the nineteenth century onwards in the theology of the Church's office as a replacement of the twofold view of office (sanctifying and leading). In this context, the discussion was about the threefold *potestas* based on Christ's giving the apostles their misisonary task.

Finally, it has also been used in ecclesiology to indicate the tasks of the Church as a whole. The canonist G. Phillips (+ 1871) did this within a view of the Church as *Christus prolongatus*, in which the participation of all Christians in Christ's three tasks takes place in a strictly hierarchical manner from the vantage-point of the head, Peter. Vatican II also employed the scheme ecclesiologically, but, unlike Phillips, affirmed that the participation of all believers in the threefold task of Christ is based on baptism (see *Lumen Gentium* 31).

(c) More Precise Definition of the Schema

These analyses and distinctions are important, not only because they make the differences in use clear, but also because they draw attention to the fact that the ecclesiological use is an extension either of the theological/anthropological use or of the use in the theology of the Church's office. The ecclesiological use cannot be combined with the other two, because their basis (baptism and mission respectively) and therefore also their resulting views of the Church are fundamentally different. In the first case, the Church is seen as the community of all the baptised. In the second, it is seen as the hierarchy with collaborators.[9]

In the light of what has previously been said about the genesis of *Lumen Gentium*, it should be clear that this second, clericalistic view of the Church was not that of the Second Vatican Council. What is more, the conception of the hierarchy as a ministry to the community is certainly not in accordance with this second view. And, if we opt for an ecclesiological use as an extension of a theological/anthropological use, it would be better to conduct the discussion of the Church's office in different terms, in order to avoid confusion. The fact that this is not the case in *Lumen Gentium* and this is one of the reasons why the text is ambivalent.[10] The schema is also employed ecclesiologically in the *Codex* and this use is in fact an extension of the theological/anthropological use. In the first canon of Book II, the People of God (204, § 1), Christian believers are defined with reference to their baptised state. On the basis of their baptism, they share in Christ's threefold task.[11] In the next canon, which deals with membership of the Catholic Church, baptism is also the basis of that membership and the link is specified in terms that call the threefold task to mind.[12]

(d) Dignity[13]

The decision to express what is common to all with the help of this schema used in theological/anthropology implies that the dignity of every baptised Christian is central in the community. This dignity has two aspects. The first is man's new being in Christ—in other words, his re-creation or *deification*. The second is that certain functions, tasks, rights and duties are connected with that new existence. This aspect, which was stressed by Vatican II,[14] provides the basis for speaking about the power and authority of all believers within the framework of the priestly, prophetic and royal character of all Christians. Because this is not self-evident, the meaningfulness and the possibilities of speaking in this way have to be demonstrated.

4. COMPETENCE

Reflection about power and authority at this universal level of the dignity of every Christian is a complex process. This it not only because there are very many different approaches to the question of power and authority, but also because the other level of power and authority in the Church—that of the ministry of the hierarchy—is almost automatically bound to play a part in this reflection. A sensible way of overcoming these complexities is to use the term 'competence' and to provide a 'conceptual' analysis of that term.[15]

(a) A Brief Analysis

Our everyday use of the term in such statements as 'she is competent' would seem to indicate that 'competence' is a person or a quality. A more detailed analysis, however, reveals that there are two ways of indicating things and qualities. There are absolute and there are relative indicators. The first draw attention to the thing or the quality itself or to the person himself. The second draw attention to something or somebody else and also only mean something in that relationship. Proper names or descriptions of colour, form or disposition can be regarded as examples of absolute indicators. Examples of relative indicators are 'neighbour', 'girlfriend', 'servant', 'in love' and 'angry'. 'Competence' belongs to the second category, because a relationship is always implied.

There are at least two kinds of relationship involved whenever we consider the places of a relationship, in other words, whenever we look at the persons or things concerned in the relationship. In such cases as 'she loves him' or 'he can see a spot', there is a relationship with two places. In a case such as 'she gives something to him', on the other hand, what we have is a relationship with two places.

'Being competent' would seem to be a relationship of two places and in particular a relationship between two persons. But it often happens that Person A is competent for Person B and that the opposite is also the case. A doctor is, for example, competent for a patient in the sphere of the diagnosis of the latter's illness. The patient, a fitter, is, however, competent for the doctor in the sphere of the diagnosis of problems with the engine of the latter's car. The sphere to which competence refers, then, also forms part of the relationship, with the result that there is a relationship of three places in the case of competence.

Two other aspects of competence can also be seen clearly in the light of what I have just said. The first is that no one is competent for himself. If he were, this would imply a negation of the relational character. The second is that there can be no question of 'absolute' competence, in other words, that someone is therefore competent for anyone else in all spheres. This is clear from the fact that, in the very wide sphere of feelings and experiences, the one who has those feelings or experiences is competent with regard to all others.

(b) The Competence of Christian Believers

This basic structure of competence makes it clear that it is both meaningful and relevant to consider the priestly, prophetic and royal character of every believer in these terms. It is a concept that is, because of the relational character outlined above, appropriate at the level of the community. Because the relationship is one of three places, the sphere—which is in this case three spheres—is a necessary part of competence. Because no one can be said to be competent for himself and because absolute competence is not a meaningful concept, competence not only presupposes a previously existing pattern of relationships, but also implies that relationships have to be built up and extended. It is only in that continuing process that everyone's competence is taken seriously and limited. Finally, any reflection about everyone's competence also implies that it is both meaningful and possible to reflect about growth in and gradation and differentiation within competence, including a more precise specification according to one or more spheres.

5. CONCLUSION

I have tried in this article to indicate the ecclesiological framework within which we should be thinking about power and authority in the Church in keeping with Vatican II. I know, of course, that, both at the level of thought and at that of structure, a great deal of work has still to be done if this initial attempt is to be developed and fully realised. I know, however, from my own experience that many believers are becoming more and more conscious of their dignity as Christians and of the competence that is associated with this and I know too that this process will continue.

Translated by David Smith

Notes

1. See John Paul II Apostolic Constitution *Sacrae Disciplinae Leges* in the 1983 edition of the *Codex* p. xi. For a survey of various pronouncements made by John Paul II about the connection between the *Codex* and the Council, see H. Schmitz 'Wertungen des Codex Iuris Canonici. Versuch einer ersten Balanz', *Archiv für katholisches Kirchenrecht* (1985) 19–57, 20–27.

2. See H. Pottmeyer, 'Vers une nouvelle phase de réception de Vatican II. Vingt ans d'herméneutique du Concile' in G. Alberigo and J. P. Jossua eds. *La réception de Vatican II* (Paris 1985) pp. 43–64. See also his 'Kontinuität und Innovation in der Ekklesiologie des II. Vatikanums. Der Einfluß des I. Vatikanums auf die Ekklesiologie des II. Vatikanums und die Neurezeption des I. Vatikanums im Lichte des II. Vatikanums' in G. Alberigo, Y. Congar and H. Pottmeyer eds. *Kirche im Wandel. Eine kritische Zwischenbalanz nach dem Zweiten Vatikanum* (Düsseldorf 1982) pp. 89–110. See also W. Kasper, 'Die bleibende Herausforderung durch das II. Vatikanischen Konzil. Zur Hermeneutik der Konzilaussagen' in WW. Kasper *Theologie und Kirche* (Mainz 1987) pp. 290–299 and *ibid. Kirche—wohin gehst du? Die bleibende Bedeutung des II. Vatikanischen Konzils* (Paderborn 1986) especially pp. 22–32.

3. A striking example of this is the *relatio* of Cardinal Browne, *Acta Synodalia Sacrosancti Concilii Vaticani Secundi II* i 339, in which he affirmed that the division of the original chapter on the laity into two separate chapters had no great consequences for the text. One part became the basis for Chapter 2, in which the People of God and what is common to all believers are dealt with.

4. See H. Schmitz *op. cit.* 31–42.

5. See H. Müller 'Communio als kirchenrechtliches Prinzip im Codex Iuris Canonici von 1983?' in *Im Gespräch mit dem dreieinen Gott. Festschrift für Wilhelm*

Breuning (Düsseldorf 1985) pp. 481–498, 483–490. On p. 497, he refers, for the concept 'transitory solution' (*Übergangslösung*), to as many as five other authors.

6. John Paul II Apostolic Constitution *Sacrae Disciplinae Leges op. cit.* p. xii.

7. See Corecco 'Kulturelle und ekklesiologische Voraussetzungen des Codex Iuris Canonici' *Archiv für katholisches Kirchenrecht* (1983) No. 152, 23–26 and Schmitz *op. cit.* 37.

8. L. Schick *Das dreifache Amt Christi und der Kirche. Zur Entstehung und Entwicklung der Trilogien* (Frankfurt a.M. and Berne 1982).

9. 'Mission' can, of course, also be understood in the general sense and not in terms of the theology of office, but, in that case, it is no longer a question of a discussion on the basis of concrete theologies.

10. The problem of the ambiguity of Vatican II in this point is therefore not only that the *potestas* language is replaced by *munus* language, but also that a language is used that superficially sounds the same, but fundamentally means something quite different.

11. The *Codex* has in fact smoothed out another and previously mentioned problematical aspect of the use of the scheme in *Lumen Gentium*, namely the 'duplication' of *Lumen Gentium* 10 and 31. In Canon 204, § 1, the 'definition' of laity is practically taken over from *Lumen Gentium* 31, but used for *christifideles* and so to speak put in the place of *Lumen Gentium* 10.

12. This observation is problematical from the historical point of view. Corecco, *op. cit.* 3–30, points out that the criterion of 'having the Spirit of Christ', which is mentioned in *Lumen Gentium* in addition to the three bonds, is not included in this canon. (See also his observations on the charismatic gifts, 26–27.) See also Schmitz' discussion of the criticism of the absence of the pneumatic dimension in the *Codex, op. cit.* 41–42. The canon can, however, perhaps also be differently interpreted, namely in accordance with *Lumen Gentium* 14. The criterion of 'having the Spirit of Christ' has, in this case, not so much disappeared as been included in the three elements named via the anointing that forms part of baptism. See the *Ordo Baptismi Parvulorum* (1983) 32.

13. See *Lumen Gentium* 13, in which we read almost in passing; ... *ut omnes qui de Populo Dei sunt, ideoque vera dignitate christiana gaudent.* ...

14. Schick points out that the functions are emphasised; *op. cit.* 133–134, 138.

15. For this conceptual analysis, I have made us of J. M. Bochenski *Was ist Autorität. Einführung in die Logik der Autorität* (Freiburg 1974). The author provides an extensive analysis of authority and, in addition to discussing the more general elements of which use is made here, also speaks about types of authority—epistemic authority, which has to do with knowing, and deontic authority, which has to do with commanding—the negation of these two types of rationalism and anarchism, the delegation of authority, its misuse and so on. These other analyses could play an important part if what I have merely outlined here were further elaborated.

Rik Torfs

Auctoritas – potestas – jurisdictio – facultas – officium – munus: a conceptual analysis

1. INTRODUCTION

CANON 17 of the new Code of Canon Law concisely and self-confidently tells us how to interpret the rules of canon law: 'Ecclesiastical laws are to be understood according to the proper meaning of the words considered in their text and context. If the meaning remains doubtful or obscure, there must be recourse to parallel places, if there be any, to the purpose and circumstances of the law, and to the mind of the legislator'.[1]

But the resulting key notion of 'the proper meaning of the words' is scarcely free from implications, and these indeed occur in regard to the relevance of legal norms and concepts of justice. This also applies of course to the six terms which are discussed in the present article. Accordingly I divide my contribution into three parts. First, I offer a summary account of the content and function of the concept of justice. Then comes the body of the article, which consists of an analysis of the six legal terms in question. Finally, a few conclusions are drawn regarding tendencies and implications.

2. THE IDEA OF JUSTICE IN CANON LAW

For some decades the literature has very often and quite rightly examined the theological and philosophical principles of canon law. Very far into the

63

present century, a positivistic legalism had been predominant. Yet there is a drawback to the new approach. Conceptual interest in the theological dimension of canon law has far too often led to an antithesis which has deprived the essential thrust of the law of due attention. In view of this tendency, it is clear that authors stress for the most part the general aspects of canon law and legal norms, whereas they often ignore the notion of justice, the concept of canon law itself, possibly because statistical and technical aspects always look straightforward. But this approach misses the surprising strength which its very flexibility bestows on the concept of law. The actual case, and of course the modalities of time and place, affect the significance accorded a specific term. I wholeheartedly go along with Potz when he says: 'The normative meaning is not directly apparent in the legal text; it can only be arrived at by a process of argumentation from the reciprocal relationship between the text and the particular situation.'[2]

Those who devised the 1983 Code understood this to some extent. It does not seem to be the case in can. 17. Elsewhere, however, there is a firm option for flexible legal concepts. A term like *justa poena,* which appears more than twenty times in criminal law, urgently requires practical elucidation. Matrimonial law, with its considerable practical relevance, offers a substantial number of nicely formulated open legal terms such as *totius vitae consortium* (can. 1055), *defectus discretionis iudicii* (can. 1095 § 2) and *obligationes matrimonii essentiales* (can. 1095 § 3).

Furthermore, even when the legislator originally conceived a legal term in a minimally flexible manner, under the pressure of social development and in the course of time, it can nevertheless take on an open aspect. The possibility of dissolving a marriage *ratum sed non consummatum*, reluctantly conceded since Pope Alexander III (1159–1181) and still restricted by the principle of indissolubility, would seem to offer new perspectives. This is all the more so because the legal term *consummatio* is being slowly liberated from a once seemingly self-evident biological frame of reference. According to can. 1061 § 1 CIC 1983 a marriage is ratified and consummated when the parties have performed between themselves the conjugal act *humano modo*. At the same time, an opportunity has been afforded for interpretation of the concept *consummatio*, even though for the lay person the meaning would seem to have been absolutely fixed for some centuries.[3]

The foregoing shows how very changeable a legal term can be after all, with a current significance different from what was originally intended by the lawgiver. With the above in mind, we can now move on to a practical analysis of the terms associated with power in the Church.

3. AUCTORITAS, POTESTAS, IURISDICTIO, FACULTAS, MUNUS, OFFICIUM

(a) Auctoritas

The term *auctoritas* occurs very often in the Code of Canon Law. It appears more than fifty times as an isolated concept. It is even more often met with as part of set expressions. We frequently come up against *auctoritas competens, auctoritas ecclesiastica competens* and, less often, *auctoritas competens Ecclesiae*: the three expressions together occur more than a hundred times. For that matter, in the process no major demarcations are established between them. The term *auctoritas* also occurs in other expressions.[4]

In most cases *auctoritas* refers to government. Though it may be justifiable to ask about the appropriateness of the excessive use of the term within the Church, there seems to be no need for profound distrust of the concept in this instance. *Auctoritas* may refer to government but it is not a term implying that the rule in question is authoritarian by nature, by reason of the prevalent common approximation in ordinary discourse of the terms *auctoritas* and 'authoritarian'. *Auctoritas*, of itself and when used in the sense of government, is a neutral term. If *auctoritas civilis* is referred to, then all sorts and conditions of possession of authority arc involved, irrespective of whether the authority in question is exercised in a democratic manner.

Of course complete innocence is seldom met with. Precisely because the Code of Canon Law acknowledges certain possibilities as such in people or institutions, it affords them a certain legitimacy. Authority is power which the legal system recognises as legal.[5] Authority which relies on legitimate power always carries with it a risk of the misuse of power and, in certain cases, lust for power. But such a risk is attached to all forms of authority. This is not specific to the Church.

In addition to 'government', *auctoritas* has yet another acceptation in the Code. The term also refers, more directly, to due authority and may then be translated as 'authority' pure and simple, in the sense of 'on the authority of'. No major distinction should be made between *auctoritas* in the sense of 'government' and in the sense of 'authority'. The second acceptation is derived from the first. When someone exercises a particular authority of office, specific decisions are associated with it.

(b) Potestas

The term *potestas* also occurs often in the Code of Canon Law. In its pure and simple form, it is met with more than eighty times and it also occurs regularly in composite forms.[6] *Potestas* is very often used in connection with the power of governance or jurisdiction in the Church, the so-called *potestas regiminis*, which is described in general terms in cann. 129 to 144 of book I. As canon 135, § 1 puts it, the power of governance or jurisdiction is distinguished as legislative, executive and judicial power. There is an implicit comparison with the *trias politica* of Montesquieu, which nowadays in an adapted form, is for the most part a cornerstone of the constitution of western democracies. It cannot be denied that this draws inspiration from civil law. Can. 135 CIC 1983 is new: in CIC 1917 there is no more than a very embryonic mention of a distinction or division of powers.[7] Here again, however, we have to do with a civil influence which is more formal than practical. Can. 135 acknowledges no real distribution of powers, for all it really does it to spread the power of jurisdiction over three areas, which always come under the control of the same instances.

The term *potestas*, in the context of a description of various aspects of the power of governance, is a technical term which is also used in civil law (power, *Macht, pouvoir*) without negative connotations. It is apposite to inquire if this terminology of civil law is referred to in the Code. Surely it is all too clear a reflection of the image of the Church as a *societas perfecta*? The adoption of secular legal terminology is not so much a matter of introducing the notion of the distribution of power obtaining in secular constitutional law as with the division into three 'powers', yet that notion quite fails to appear in canon law. The citation of the *potestas regiminis* with its division into three traditional powers can be much more a matter of the implicit manifestation of universal ideas and fundamental concepts than a specific concern with the usage for its own sake. The latter, if there is an option for a form of *trias politica* in the Church, is mere tidiness.

This does not always seem to be the case when the term *potestas*, scattered here and there in the Code, is a loosely attached concept. Its use seems quite irreproachable when power is used in the general sense of the faculties which someone possesses to exploit possibilities inherent in power. *Potestas* is only sporadically apparent in that acceptation in the Code.[8]

The term occurs much more often when there is talk of the competences of specific individuals and instances. There is ample and plain citation of the 'power' enjoyed by the Pope. I quote as an example the beginning of can. 333, § 1: 'By virtue of his office, the Roman Pontiff not only has power over the universal Church, but also has pre-eminent ordinary power over all particular Churches and their groupings'.[9]

Moreover the power of other persons is clearly stressed. There is an exemplary reference to the potestas of the diocesan bishop,[10] of religious superiors,[11] of the episcopal vicar.[12] It is clear that what is referred to is *potestas regiminis*.

In all these examples, I find the term *potestas* inappropriate. In the case of the Pope, for instance, *auctoritas* (authority) is preferable, certainly if it is assumed, as I suggested in the foregoing, that authority or competence is a power which the order of justice acknowledges as legal or legitimate. Similarly, in a number of cases I would replace *potestas* with *facultas* (competence proper). The competence of the diocesan bishop or of a religious superior is judicially purer than his or her power. *Potestas* is a term I would use only when the association with *potestas regiminis* is directly demonstrable, when in other words there is a direct reference to the power of jurisdiction or governance in the general or direct sense in one of its three aspects. I should not wish to use it for an isolated part aspect cited in a legal provision.

(c) Iurisdictio

The term *iurisdictio* occurs only five times in the new Code. In the first section regarding jurisdictional power or the power of governance, the famous can. 129, *potestas iurisdictionis* is abandoned as a synonym for *potestas regiminis*. It is however this latter expression which the Code regularly uses. *Iurisdictio*, according to can. 129, is used only the sense of 'power of governance'.[13]

(d) Facultas

Facultas, in contradistinction to *iurisdictio*, is a term which is repeatedly enlisted by the Code. It is met with in its own right some seventy times, very often in the application of 'competence'.

Altogether, *facultas* has four applications in the present Code: (i) faculty for instruction; (ii) possibility/opportunity; (iii) ability or capacity; (iv) competence.[14] Only the last of these senses is relevant to the purposes of the present article.

Facultas (competence) is in distinct competition with *potestas* (power) in the Code. In a couple of instances that emerges clearly. See, for instance, cann. 1079 and 1080 CIC 1983, which are concerned with power (or competence ...) to dispense from forms prescribed for and from (occult) impediments to the celebration of marriage. Whenever there is talk of an appropriate faculty in the course of these definitions, it is always of *potestas dispensandi*. Why? The preparatory works offer no explanation. Certainly it was intended to emphasise the association with the power of jurisdiction. The power to dispense belongs to the *potestas regiminis delegata* (delegated power) in the sense of can. 131, § 1 CIC 1983.

Of course, the concern here is with details, but they are significant. Clearly, in the wake of *potestas regiminis*, there is an excessive option for the term *potestas*, which is inferior on legally technical grounds to *facultas* (see *infra*); it also implies that a power of jurisdiction cannot be derived other than by using the term *potestas*. Why is it impossible to distinguish the practical expression of an aspect of *potestas regiminis* in terms of the notion of *facultas*?

Meanwhile, we should not forget that *facultas* in the sense of competence is not so widespread in the Code. It is to be found more in descriptions of the competences of the legate,[15] the chaplain,[16] the canon penitentiary,[17] and the pastor,[18] so that it attaches not so much to persons as to functions, from the faculty to preach everywhere,[19] to confirmation,[20] and to the faculty to exercise a power of absolution.[21]

It is also interesting to note in some cases the citation of *potestas* and of *facultas* close together. This is the case, for instance in can. 409 § 2, which is concerned with the 'powers and faculties' of an auxiliary bishop *sede vacante*;and in cann. 527 § 2 and 543 § 1, mention is made of the 'powers and faculties' of the pastor. In general, it is safe to assume that power is an amount or instance of jurisidictional power, both acquired and delegated,[22] whereas competence is neither associated legally with an office, nor delegated, but is acquired. Hence, in addition to the rights and duties accorded to him by the Code, the deacon can also possess competences or faculties which are accorded to him by the particular right.[23]

Even though it is a basis for distinguishing between *potestas* and *facultas*, so that the former is associated with the power of jurisdiction whereas the latter term is not legally associated with an office (*officium*), the distinction seems too artificial. *Potestas* should be restricted rather as a term to the abstract description of jurisdictional power, whereas there should be more mention of *facultas* as a juridically legitimated *potestas*.

(e) Officium

The term *officium* occurs in CIC 1983 some 260 times. A number of these instances have little to do with *officium* as an office, except as mentioned hereinafter. In the Code *officium* also refers to:

(i) duty. This acceptation occurs some sixty times. It then functions almost as a synonym for *obligatio*, as is clearly shown by can. 793, § 1 on Catholic education. First the conjunction is made between *obligatio* and *ius*, and a little later *officium* and *ius* are equated.

(ii) service, in the sense of care of, e.g., a religious community.[24]

(iii) service or office in the sense of an institution.[25]

(iv) office in the sense of secrecy of office, when the reference is to secrecy in regard to, e.g., secular individuals.[26]

By far most references in the Code of Canon Law are to *officium* in the sense of ecclesiastical office. Title IX of Book I refers to it and in can. 145 § 1 we find a definition: 'An ecclesiastical office is any function constituted in a stable manner, by divine or ecclesiastical law to be exercised for a spiritual purpose'. Thus an *officium* is characteristically defined by a clear and specific content.

Officium is often used correctly in the sense of can. 145, for instance when it is a question of defining distance from an office. More than in other instances, here the Code seems to deviate from its usual attention to its own definitions. I shall restrict myself to two significant instances where *munera* would have been more appropriate:

(i) can. 230 § 3. In certain cases when ministers are lacking, lectors or acolytes can supply for certain of their offices;

(ii) can. 395 § 2. The bishop has a duty of residence. One of the just causes for his absence can be *officii sibi legitime commissi* (time spent on another office which has been legitimately entrusted to him).

(f) Munus

The term *munus* functions on a macro and on a micro plane in CIC 1983. On the macro level the term *munus* has an essential role in the determination of the structure of the Code. It starts with a book on general norms and closes with the temporal goods, and criminal and case law. The intermediate three books are divided in accordance with the three traditional *munera* which occur in the Church, namely *munus regendi* (not mentioned by name in the title of Book II), *munus docendi* (Book III) and *munus sanctificandi* (Book IV). The three traditional *munera* are the authentic 'three powers' in the Church. Whereas the separation from *potestas regiminis* as in can. 135 § 1, occurs throughout the Code, not much more than a fascinating 'fait divers' is involved; but the three *munera* show that they are of cardinal importance for the structure of the entire Code. *Munus* does not refer to a specific office but to major tasks which operate also through offices. A *munus*, or macro level, is a task in the sense of Mission; the latter term is understood existentially, and possibly accorded an initial capital letter.

On the micro level, *munus* may also be translated as 'task', but the term is much more limited in application. It is not a key term which implicitly ordains the division of the entire Code, but (for the rest in an inferior position) refers to 'state', as opposed to the 'office' implied by the term *officium*. *Munus* is not closely elucidated as a concept but recourse to the definition of *officium* throws light on both *officium* and *munus*. In that context, an ecclesiastical office (*officium*) permanently constitutes every task (*munus*), in virtue of its divine and ecclesiastical law, as that which is to be exercised for a spiritual purpose. This definition allows of two far from excessively daring conclusions:

(a) An *officium* is a *munus* enjoying special authority, subject to specific conditions. Every *officium* is a *munus* but the contrary is not necessarily true.

(b) Inasmuch as the stable condition of an *officium* distinguishes it from a *munus*, similarly it may be concluded that a *munus* is less rigidly structured. It is a more open legal notion and may be creatively shaped.

Another less directly deducible implication of the definition is the following. An *officium* which in accordance with canon 145 § 2, involves various rights and duties, can also consist of a number of separate *munera*. The office of bishop for instance includes multiple tasks.

Munus on the macro level is a major task, a Mission of the Church, and *officia* may assist towards the fulfilment of that purpose. The same *officia* comprehend one or more stable micro tasks. Moreover, apart from *officia* there are tasks which are less precisely defined than the former.

This seemingly logically acceptable division does not however wholly suit the practical usage of the Code. The term *munus* occurs less than two hundred times. In many of these instances it appears in the application 'task'.

More than once the term *munus* occurs when the use of *officium* seems also indicated as eligible. Some examples:

– can. 377 § 2 speaks of episcopal *munus*;
– can. 331 repeatedly refers to the papacy as *munus*;
– can. 430 § 11 treats of a *munus* of diocesan administrator;
– can. 617 speaks of superiors of Institutes and their *munus*;
– can. 1445 § 1 allows of a *munus* for auditors of the Roman Rota.

Thus: *munus* and *officium* should be interchanged in a number of instances in the Code of Canon Law.

4. CONCLUSIONS

(a) Power, an Unattractive Term?

In the foregoing I have examined various terms which all have to do with power and authority. Within the Church there does not seem to be a deep concern for open elucidation of such terms. Canon lawyers and those in authority are anxious to explain that power has to be understood as service, yet theologians deplore the fact that in the Code there is more talk of power than of *amor*. The latter term occurs only six times.

In my opinion, the score of six here is too high and there is no need to be ashamed of such terms as competence and authority. Whereas love in all its elusive beauty on the legal level is a very open but also an extremely manipulable concept, terms such as *auctoritas* and *facultas* contribute to the establishment of precise contexts and permissible expectations. The religious aspect is soemthing secure; open legal terms refer to an area between illusion and reality, and even to the impossible, and perhaps also undesirable.

I conclude that a terminology to do with authority and competence may of course not express the very essence of what the Church is about, yet may help to describe the boundaries of possibility when love is cold and the Code of Canon Law has to be consulted for consolation.

(*b*) Discussion of Power within the Present Church Structures

It is therefore not incorrect to say that in regard to *auctoritas* the Code uses cognate terms. Evidently this occurs frequently.It is very regrettable that there should be so consistent a treatment of 'powers' and 'competences' within a system in which there is scarcely any trace of a distribution of authority. To be sure, the Church's own authority makes possible the adoption of a secular system of division of powers. But on the other hand, the spreading of authority can be used to cover abuses of authority at the heart of the Church, abuses which even a Church cannot wholly escape by virtue of its elevated mission. The full implications of the *trias politica* are rejected, but an independent legal power must certainly raise the level of the system.[27]

I am convinced that the concentration of power in the Church has had a direct influence on the development, quality and interpretation of the concept of justice in CIC 1983.

Careless usage is possible only if there is not a complete dissociation of legislative from judicial instances, if genuine interpretation can or may not be entirely free. Only a legislator who is not subject to real external inquiry can tolerate with impunity inaccuracies such as those on the borderline between *officium* and *munus*, or indistinct boundaries like those between *facultas* and *potestas* or between *officium* and *obligatio*.

The careless formulation of the Code results once again in legal terminology which betrays its very clearly open character, even when it is not consciously formulated in an open manner.

None of the terms discussed in this article is so rigidly fixed that it exercises an immovable influence within the Church—with some slight reservation in the case of *potestas*, which is often used in far too inflated a way, for instance in the direct context of *potestas regiminis*.

The lack of a quite consistently enacted division of powers produces careless usage and consequently a considerable number of manifestly open legal terms. May we therefore conclude that the concentration of power (and associated disadvantages) nevertheless stimulates a healthy evolution of the concept of justice? The answer is No. The concentration of power cuts both ways. In theory it allows room for the interpretation of authority, but in practice the result is that judicial power and the supreme *potestas regiminis* remain concentrated in the same persons and instances, so that a traditional interpretation of many key terms is more appropriate. That is certainly the case in areas with a direct association at a high level with Church government and policy. In other areas there is a degree of room for action which allows of a certain optimism. I refer here to fields which either *ratione materiae* (e.g., matrimonial law) or *ratione loci* (e.g., private law) fall outside the immediate location of interest of the organs of central government.

In practice this means that bishops, who possess the due *potestas* (or ought one rather to say *facultas*?) in their dioceses, can use different terms—amongst others the open legal notion *munus*—in extreme bids to overturn structures which answer local needs.

A few words in conclusion. Some legal terms associated with power and authority are defined in the Code, for instance *officium* and in a certain sense the dangerous and ambiguous *potestas*, but most terms are not thus elucidated. More often, when a definition does appear it is not consistent with other instances throughout the Code. This is a luxury which a legislator can only now afford in the absence of an independent judiciary which can call him to account when his work is inadequate. A consequence of careless usage however is an enhancement of the quite open character of legal terminology, so that especially at the micro level policy-makers and judges can do something—creatively—to form and open up the law.

Translated by J. G. Cumming

Notes

1. All quotations are from Code of Canon Law (the Latin/English edition of the Canon Law Society of America) (Washington 1983).
2. R. Potz 'Rechtsbegrip en voortgaande rechtsontwikkeling in de Codex Iuris Canonici van 1983' in *Concilium*, 23 (1986) No. 3, 26.
3. I have examined this topic in some detail in my thesis: R. Torfs, Het canonieke huwelijksbegrip (Leuven 1987), cviii + 976 pp. 000.
4. E.g., in *auctoritas Ecclesiae, ecclesiastica, Episcopi, legitima, Ordinarii, suprema. Auctoritas civilis* also appears here and there.
5. Cf. in *potestas regiminis, executiva, legislativa, iudicialis, iurisdictionis, delegata, ordinis, ordinaria, ecclesiastica, civilis, administrativa.*
6. See W. van Gervenn *Met recht en rede* (Tielt 1987) 234.

7. H. Müller 'Die Diözesankurie' in Listl, J., Müller, H. and Schmitz, H. *Handbuch des katholischen Kirchenrechts* (Regensburg 1983) 365.

8. See, e.g., cann. 747 § 1 (*qualibet humana potestate*); 1057 § 1 and 1141 (*nulla humana potestate*).

9. Other examples are to be found in e.g., cann. 331 and 332 § 1.

10. See e.g., can. 427 § 1 (*religiosi subsunt potestati Episcoporum*); 1423 § 1; 1439 § 3.

11. Cann. 596 § 1; 596 § 3; 615; 617; 620 ...

12. Can. 479 § 2.

13. See can. 1417 § 2; 1469 § 1 (2x); 1512 § 3.

14. Instruction: e.g., can. 229; 253 § 1; 809, 815, 816 ... Possibility: can. 695 § 2; 697 § 2°; 1569 § 1;1720 § 1°. Ability: can. 799. Competence: throughout.

15. Can. 364 § 8°.

16. Can. 566 § 1.

17. Can. 508 § 1.

18. E.g., can. 510 § 2.

19. Can. 764.

20. Cann. 882; 883; 884 § 1; 884 § 2; 885 § 2; 887.

21. Cann. 966 § 1; 966 § 2; 967 § 2; 967 § 3; 974 § 2; 974 § 4; 975.

22. Cf. can. 131 § 1.

23. Can. 555 § 1.

24. Can. 556.

25. Can. 1733 § 2 and 3, also canon 775 § 3.

26. Can. 1455 § 1; 1548 § 2, 1°.

27. This point has also been made in a Justice and Peace Commission document: *Mensenrechten in de Kerk* (Brussels 1986) 77 pp. 000.

Augustine Mendonca

Proper and Vicarious Power in the Church
What does this Distinction Mean?

INTRODUCTION

AT VATICAN II the Church attempted to set forth its own nature and universal mission.[1] Instead of describing itself as a 'perfect society', as Vatican I did, the Church calls itself a 'mystery', a 'sacrament', a 'communion', 'body of Christ', 'People of God', etc. In this way the Council tried to explain the 'complex reality' of the Church, made up of divine and human elements, and to shed light on some of the most important issues concerning the nature of the Church.

One of these issues is the distinction between the *proper* and *vicarious* power of the Church. The emergence of these theologico-canonical concepts and the underlying distinction between them is the result of a long historical development.[2] This development has not been without controversy. Authors differ concerning the meaning of 'proper' and 'vicarious' power.

According to F. M. Cappello, for example, the proper power of the Church is that 'which *necessarily and essentially* belongs to the Church as *a truly perfect society* so that it *connaturally* follows its existence and nature; therefore, it is exercised by the Church *in its own name* as in its proper sphere of activity'.[3] 'Vicarious power is that which is granted to the Church *in virtue of a special commission*; therefore, it belongs to the Church only to the extent it is

74

God's instrument and carries out His ministry; consequently, it exercises this power *in the name of God*. In virtue of this power,the Church infallibly declares the word of God, dissolves a sacramental and non-consummated marriage, etc.'[4]

These definitions circumscribe the sphere of proper power of the Church to legislative, judicial and executive or coercitive powers of jurisdiction which pertain to it as a 'perfect society'; vicarious power includes the power of order, power of teaching, and the remaining portion of the power of jurisdiction which comprises the power to remit sins, to grant indulgences, to dispense from vows, oaths and sacramental marriages.[5]

Other authors restrict vicarious power to the power of jurisdiction alone. Thus, for example, according to F. X. Wernz, vicarious power is that power of jurisdiction 'which is granted to the Church in virtue of a *special commission* and exercised by it *in the forum of God*. By reason of this vicarious power, it infallibly declares the *word of God*, remits sins, grants indulgences, dispenses from vows, oaths and sacramental marriages'.[6] The power of order included within the sphere of vicarious power in the previous definition is excluded in this definition. More recent canonists often tend to restrict the concept of vicarious power even further. For example, F. Lambruschini states: 'By the term *vicarious power*, authors indicate that power of the Roman Pontiff by which he dispenses from obligations arising either from a vow, or from an oath, or from a marriage which is "only sacramental" or legitimate'.[7]

In this brief study, an attempt will be made to answer two basic questions. First, what does the distinction between 'proper' and 'vicarious' power mean? Second, is this distinction still relevant or valid in light of Vatican II ecclesiology?

1. HISTORICAL EVOLUTION OF THE CONCEPTS

An important distinction must be kept in mind to understand the evolution of the concepts of 'proper' and 'vicarious' power and their underlying distinction.[8] The *exercise* of power is distinct from the *concept* of power. The exercise of power is possible without theorising about the distinction in the power granted to the Church by Christ. The scope of the exercise of power depends on concrete pastoral circumstances of time and place, and on the self-awareness the Church has of the extent of its powers.

The Church has always been conscious of the fact that Christ endowed it with the fullness of power necessary to actualise his mission on earth. The awareness of the extent of this power has been gradual. Thus, from the beginning the Church exercised the power of governing the faithful, proclaiming infallibly the word of God, administering sacraments, and more gradually granting indulgences, dispensing from vows, oaths, and dissolving certain types of marriages.[9]

(a) Evolution of the Concept of 'Vicarious Power'

From the early years of the Church the term 'vicarious power', borrowed from Roman Law, signified the fullness of power the Church received from Christ and exercised in his name. The Fathers of the Church called the entire power of the Church *divine*, meaning it is from Christ and exercised in his name to fulfil his mission on earth. This power was always regarded as one.

During the medieval period there was an intense theologico-canonical reflection on the nature of the Church's power. The first distinction that emerged as a result of these reflections was between power and its execution. In ordination a person received the fullness of power necessary for the pastoral care of souls, but its execution needed legitimate commission from competent authority. Further analysis led to the distinction between power of order and power of jurisdiction. The criterion for the distinction was the origin of these powers; the source of the power of order was ordination, and that of the power of jurisdiction was the positive act of a competent superior, or in the case of the Roman Pontiff, the very act of acceptance of election. This distinction of powers of the Church reflected a profound change in the unitary concept of ecclesial power present in the first millenium and prepared the way for the specific concept of vicarious power in subsequent centuries.

The development of the theory on ministers of the sacraments as instrumental causes also occurred during the medieval period. Thomas Aquinas (1225–1274) applied the theory of instrumental causality[10] explicitly only to sacramental actions and not to signify vicarious power as propounded by later canonists. During and following the pontificate of Innocent III (1198–1216) there emerged theories that the Roman Pontiff, as the 'Vicar of Christ', could dispense from certain bonds of natural law or any other bonds including those pertaining to external ecclesiastical society and even those pertaining to civil society. This theory was clearly expressed in the papal bull *Unam sanctam*, 18 November 1302 of Boniface VIII (1294–1303).[11]

There was no explicit indication of the distinction between 'proper power' and 'vicarious power' in the developments that took place during the medieval period. All power in the Church was regarded as vicarious, that is from Christ and exercised by the Church in his name. Whatever power the Roman Pontiff exercised was considered divine and from God. Even the power of dissolving a marriage was God's power exercised by the Roman Pontiff as His Vicar. The vicarious role of the Pope was not understood in the restrictive sense which developed during the post-reformation period.

The concept of vicarious power restricted to the sphere of jurisdiction and contradistinguished from 'proper power', was a development of the modern period. During this period, attempts were made to answer some subtle questions concerning the Pope's power to dispense from natural law obligations, more specifically his power to dissolve the marriage bond. In response to this situation, a twofold distinction emerged between obligations of natural law deriving from human will, such as a vow, an oath, and those arising from divine will.[12] The marriage bond was added to the group of obligations deriving from human will. The theory behind this development implied that the Roman Pontiff had the fullness of power from Christ in governing the Church and is in the place of God on earth. In dissolving these bonds, he would be acting not as a human being but as God, not by human but divine authority.

In the meantime, another characteristic connoting the concept of 'vicarious power' emerged in theological reflections. Vicarious power was given to the Church by Christ by a special commission. In resolving a dispute over the nature of papal power to transfer a bishop from his diocese which, according to the prevalent doctrine, involved dissolution of the spiritual bond between the bishop and his diocese, Pope Innocent III had declared that the power to transfer a bishop was the prerogative of Christ alone; nevertheless, it was given to Peter and his successors by a 'special privilege'. Innocent III in fact did not use the expression 'by a special commission' (*ex speciali commissione*), nor did he state that this power was 'extraordinary' as claimed by canonists of later centuries. He probably meant that according to the mentality of the time, the transfer of a bishop from his diocese was reserved to the Pope and it was a special 'privilege'.[13]

The idea of 'special commission' related to the Pope's power to dispense from the obligations of natural law was probably derived from the principle underlying dispensation from human laws. An inferior cannot dispense from his superior's laws without a 'special commission'. When this principle is univocally applied to dispensation from divine natural laws it would read: the Pope can dispense from the laws of God in virtue of a 'special commission'. This 'special commission' is implicit in his office as the visible head of the Church, the 'Vicar of Christ'. In virtue of this special commission, he could remove a divine law obligation through a real dispensation in a particular case for an urgent cause.[14] At the time when this concept emerged, it simply meant that the Roman Pontiff, by virtue of his office, had the power to dispense from not abrogate or derogate, certain natural law obligations.

Toward the end of the fifteenth century the concepts of 'proper power of jurisdiction' as opposed to 'vicarious power of jurisdiction' began to crystallise. Three distinct historic facts seem to have influenced this process: first, the demise of the theory which advocated the extension of papal power over all people and nations; second, the evolution of an ecclesiology which defined the Church as a 'perfect society' similar to constitutionally monarchic civil societies; third, impoverishment of the theology of vicarious power and its juridicisation.[15] As a result, the power of the Roman Pontiff lost its rich, sacred and theological significance and became more human; it was expressed more in juridical terms borrowed from civil and international laws. The Pope became one among several heads of State. As a consequence, the concept of 'Vicar of Christ' was deprived of the rich theological meaning attributed to it by medieval theologians and canonists. Neither the Council of Trent nor Vatican I made any direct reference to the title of 'Vicar of Christ' or of 'vicarious power' even though the supremacy of the papal power or of jurisdiction and papal infallibility were proclaimed solemnly.

Thus in the final stage of its evolution the concept of 'vicarious power' became completely devoid of its original meaning and was restricted to that power by which bonds of natural law arising from human will (vows, oaths, certain marriages) were dissolved, or according to some, also the power to remit sins, grant indulgences and declare the word of God infallibly. The theoretical explanation of the nature of the power to dissolve those bonds also was bereft of any profound meaning. Juridic elements of ecclesial power received maximum attention to the neglect of relevant theological elements. In this process, therefore, the concept of 'vicarious power' was reduced to the concept of 'power of jurisdiction' granted by Christ to the Roman Pontiff by a special commission, distinct from the 'power of jurisdiction' which is proper to the Church as a 'perfect society'.

(b) Evolution of the Concept of 'Proper Power'

Two distinct concepts of 'proper power' are identifiable in the history of its development. These may be designated as: 'extra-ecclesial concept' of proper power and 'intra-ecclesial concept' of proper power.[16]

The 'extra-ecclesial concept' of proper power addresses the relationship between Church and State. Two conceptually different periods can be distinguished in its evolution: a period of 'societary monism' and a period of 'societary dualism'.

During the period of 'societary monism', which spanned from the early years of the Church to the sixteenth century, the notion of one 'Christian republic' or one 'perfect community' prevailed. In this republic, two distinct powers were exercised: the power of the secular head of the republic and that of the spiritual head. Thus, for example, in 494 Pope Gelasius I (492–496) expressed this distinction to defend the independence of the spiritual power from the secular power. In his letter to emperor Anasthasius I (491–518), Gelasius wrote the famous dictum: 'There are two persons, august emperor, by whom this world is principally governed: the sacred authority of pontiffs and the royal power'.[17]

The gelasian doctrine on temporal and spiritual powers provided the foundation for medieval theories on the separation of powers and on the relationship between Church and State. The domain of spiritual power would be to excommunicate, to absolve from sins, to grant indulgences, etc., whereas the State would decide on issues related to property, to judge, to impose capital punishment or to pardon from such punishment, to levy taxes, etc. According to medieval theories, therefore, entire spiritual power comprising the power of orders and jurisdiction would be proper to the Church in opposition to the powers of the State. At this time the notion of 'society' had not become the criterion of distinction between Church and State and between their powers. There was one 'perfect community' with two powers exercised independently from each other.

With the emergence of national States in Europe from the sixteenth century, the dualistic concept of 'perfect society' replaced the monistic concept of 'perfect community'. The Church and the State upheld their autonomy and independence by claiming that each one was a 'perfect society' and, consequently, had its proper sphere of activity and 'proper power'.[18] In this context, the sphere of proper ecclesial power became restricted to the power of jurisdiction similar to the power of a civil state. Thus the concept of 'proper power', which was much broader in its connotation, became identified with 'proper jurisdiction'.

One of the important issues severely criticized by Protestant reformers was the Church's claim to 'proper power' in opposition to the power of the state. They vigorously argued that Christian religion does not constitute a special state, a republic distinct by divine right from the civil republic. At the most it can be regarded as a 'college', a gathering of faithful on their own free will, but entirely subject to civil power in all aspects of external jurisdiction. Catholic canonists of the eighteenth century, especially those from the German speaking countries, countered the Protestant doctrine of 'collegial system' by demonstrating how absurd it would be if the Church were to be reduced to a 'college' in the State without any power of its own. They insisted, therefore, that the Church is a society similar to civil society in all aspects. Christian society is of divine origin and it is a perfect society.[19] As a monarchic republic and as a perfect society, the Church must enjoy proper power. It is a republic constituted and ordered for the purpose of attaining the supernatural salvation of souls. Its power is fundamentally spiritual and independent of all other powers. During the nineteenth century, the term 'perfect society' became technical and together with the concept of 'proper power' formed one terminological formula. This became the central thesis of treatises on public ecclesiastical law.

The 'intra-ecclesiastical concept' of proper power is contra-distinguished from the theological concept of 'instrumental' or 'ministerial' or 'vicarious' power of the Church.[20] This concept probably originates from F. Suarez (1548–1617) who considered as proper the power which the Church exercises as the principal cause, while instrumental power is that which is exercised by the Church as an instrument of Christ its head.[21] Such power consists in communicating grace or granting remission of sins. This distinction between 'proper' and 'instrumental' power was applied to legislative power for the first time by Mattheo Liberatore' (1810–1892). According to Liberatore, the Church in exercising merely legislative power which corresponds to civil power, acts as the principal cause; however, in exercising the power of teaching, it acts as an instrumental cause. This distinction broadened the sphere of instrumental jurisdiction because until then besides the power of order, only jurisdiction to remit sins belonged to instrumental power.

Louis Billot (1846–1931), for the first time called instrumental power of jurisdiction 'ministerial jurisdiction'; and considered it equivalent to all aspects of the power of order. F. X. Wernz (1842–1914) adopted the more juridic term 'vicarious jurisdiction' instead of ministerial or instrumental jurisdiction.

In 1899, the 'extra-ecclesial' and 'intra-ecclesial' concepts of proper power were so confused that from then on the 'proper power' of the Church as a 'perfect society' became identified with 'proper jurisdiction' which the Church exercises in its own name and in its proper sphere of activity as opposed to 'vicarious powers'.[22] This marked the beginning of the formulation of terminology of 'proper' and 'vicarious' power as understood in the specific modern sense found in the definitions discussed earlier. The fusion of both concepts was intended to commit the controversial 'extra-ecclesial concept' of proper power to oblivion. More recent authors have been using only the 'intra-ecclesial concept' of proper power to contradistinguish it from the concept of 'vicarious power' of the Church.[23]

2. IN LIGHT OF THE DOCTRINE OF VATICAN II

The Second Vatican Council identified certain essential characteristics of the Church which are irreconcilable with the past concepts of 'proper power' and 'vicarious power'.

First, the Council unequivocally affirmed the 'structural and organic unity' of the Church.[24] The clearest expression of this intrinsic unity is to be found in *Lumen gentium* 8: 'But, the society structured with hierarchical organs and the mystical body of Christ, the visible society and the spiritual community, the earthly Church and the Church endowed with heavenly riches are not to be thought of as two realities. On the contrary, they form one complex reality which comes together from a human and divine element.'[25]

The Council used the term 'society' several times to emphasise principally the Church's special nature which distinguishes it from other societies. In this 'society', the visible, structural and human elements are essentially united with the invisible, spiritual and charismatic elements; just as the humanity of Christ serves the Word as a living organism of salvation, similarly the 'social structure of the Church' serves the spiritual and vital elements of the Church.[26] This 'social structure' of the Church is not something standing by itself, different from the spiritual Church, but together it forms one complex reality, the Church, the People of God. Hence, all ecclesial functions and powers are at the service of the Church as a 'priestly' or 'worshipping' community.[27]

Second, the Council deliberately upheld the 'unitary' and 'sacred' nature of ecclesial powers. It shed all vestiges of the distinction between the concepts of 'proper' and 'vicarious' powers. The entire power in the Church is presented as one and sacred under the general term 'potestas sacra'.[28] Furthermore, the Council avoided any reference to the distinction between the 'power of order' and 'power of jurisdiction' even though in some conciliar texts this distinction is implicit; only once did it expressly mention the 'power of order'.[29] The unitary concept of the Church necessarily demands a unitary concept of ecclesial power because 'action proceeds from being'.

Third, the Council alluded several times to the vicarious nature of ecclesial power with the use of the term 'vicarious'. The Roman Pontiff is referred to as the 'Vicar of Christ' twice in the text of *Lumen gentium*, 18, 22, once in the *Nota Expl. Praev.* 3°, and once in *Optatam totius*, 9.[30] The term is applied also to bishops (*LG*. 27) even as members of the College of Bishops (*LG*. 21, 22). However, the concept underlying the term 'vicarious' stresses the fact that all power enjoyed by the Church is from Christ and exercised in his name. Only in this sense is ecclesial power 'vicarious' and not in the sense of a 'specially committed' power.

Fourth, the Church at Vatican II no longer considered itself a 'perfect society' poised to defend its inalienable rights against other enemy States; rather it saw itself as 'the sign and safeguard of the transcendental dimension of the human person' working together with the political community for the realisation of the 'personal vocation of man'.[31] Moreover, the Council recognised the fundamental rights of religious freedom as the ontological basis of defence of the Church's rights in a pluralistic society, safeguarding however the proper nature of its powers granted to it by Christ. In this regard international conventions, universal declarations of human rights, etc., must be viewed as fundamental safeguards for the exercise of religious freedom including the rights of the Church.[32] In light of this teaching, the concepts of 'perfect society' and 'proper power' have no further use in post-conciliar ecclesiology.

Fifth, the terms 'proper' and 'vicarious' are used several times in the new Code in relation to ecclesial power,[33] but with the exception of can. 131, § 2, these terms do not connote the same meaning attached to the concepts of 'proper' and 'vicarious' power discussed thus far. Can. 131, § 2 distinguishes the ordinary power of governance (jurisdiction) into 'proper' and 'vicarious'. This is strictly a canonical distinction. Nevertheless, a certain analogy between the meanings underlying these terms and in the concepts of 'proper' and 'vicarious' power can be identified. The ordinary 'proper' power of governance mentioned in can. 131, § 2 is that which is attached to an office which is principal, whereas the ordinary 'vicarious' power of governance belongs to an office which exists only as substitutive of the principal.[34]

The Council taught in unequivocal terms that Christ is the permanent Teacher, Priest and Pastor of the Church. Therefore the Church, the Roman Pontiff, bishops and to some extent priests can be called 'Vicars of Christ' insofar as they exercise the three functions with powers attached to them in the name of Christ and as his ministers, substitutes and helpers.[35] The terms 'proper' and 'vicarious' of can. 131, § 2 refer only to the power of governance (jurisdiction); however, the 'vicarious' power of the Church refers to the totality of 'ecclesial power bestowed on it by Christ.' This power is vicarious and proper to the Church at the same time.

CONCLUSION

The Church received the fullness of 'power' from Christ to actualise his redemptive mission in this world. It understood that in virtue of this power it could celebrate the sacraments, preach, grant indulgences, dispense from vows and oaths, dissolve the marriage bond in certain cases, and govern the faithful. During the first millenium this power in its totality was regarded as 'vicarious', i.e., from Christ and exercised in his name.

But historical, political factors, and the influence of public ecclesiastical law led to the interpretation of the nature of the Church in terms of a 'perfect society'. According to the doctrine underlying this concept, the Church possessed the same 'power of jurisdiction', namely legislative, judicial, and executive or coercive, as those enjoyed by any other civil society. These powers of jurisdiction were regarded as 'proper' to the Church in virtue of it being a 'perfect society'.

At the same time theological and canonical reflections formulated the distinction between the power of order and power of jurisdiction. The power of preaching the Word of God and other powers mentioned above were grouped under the power of jurisdiction and these were considered to have been granted to the Church by a special commission. Thus there were two subtypes in the power of jurisdiction: the first type comprised the 'proper power' which included the legislative, judicial and executive or coercive powers, and the second type consisted of the 'vicarious power' which included the power to preach, to grant indulgences, etc. While the first group belonged to the Church as 'proper' to its nature as 'perfect society' the second set of powers were granted to it by a special commission by Christ. This kind of reasoning can lead to the absurd conclusion that Christ instituted the Church primarily as a 'perfect society' endowed by its very nature with the proper power of governance while granting it the more important powers of teaching, celebrating sacraments, etc., only by a special commission. This is irreconcilable with the teaching of Vatican II. The power of the Church is one and holy and it belongs to the Church by its very institution by Christ; it is exercised by its ministers in Christ's name. Therefore, the distinctions between 'proper' and 'vicarious' power as understood in the past is not admissible in light of the ecclesiology of Vatican II. All power of the Church is both 'proper' and 'vicarious' at the same time.

Notes

1. *Lumen gentium* (= LG), 1 in *Acta Apostolicae Sedis* (= *AAS*) 57 (1965) 5.

2. See R. A. Casio 'De vicaria Ecclesiae potestate' *Ius seraphicum* 4 (1958) 591–616; 5 (1959) 56–87, 153–203, 330–366; U. Navarrete 'Potestas vicaria Ecclesiae: Evolutio historica conceptus atque observationes attenta doctrina Concilii Vaticani II' *Periodica* 60 (1971) 415–486; R. Schwarz, 'Do potestate propria Ecclesiae', *Periodica* 63 (1974) 428–445.

3. F. M. Cappello *Summa iuris publici ecclesiastici* 6th ed. (Romae: Apud Aedes Universitatis Gregorianae 1954), n. 139, p. 117 (emphasis in original).

4. *Ibid.* (emphasis in original).

5. See Navarrete p. 416.

6. F. X. Wernz *Ius decretalium* II/1, 2nd ed. (Romae, 1906), p. 13 (emphasis in original).

7. F. Lumbruschini 'Disputatio de potestate vicaria Romani Pontificis in matrimonium infidelium' *Apollinaris* 26 (1953) 178.

8. See Navarrete pp. 419–420.

9. *Ibid.* pp. 420–421.

10. See *Summa Theol.* III, q. 64, a. 5; *In IV Sent.*, d. 5, q. 2, a. 2, sol. 2 and 3; *C. Gent.* 4, 76.

11. See Denzinger-Schönmetzer *Enchiridion symbolorum* nn. 872–875.

12. See T. Sanchez *De matrimonio* lib. 8, disp. 6, n. 5.

13. See U. Navarrete p. 438.

14. See T. Sanchez lib. 8, disp. 6, n. 5.

15. See U. Navarrete pp. 442–447.

16. See R. Schwarz p. 429.

17. *Ep.* 12, 2, as quoted in R. Schwarz, p. 430.

18. See F. Suarez *Defensio fidei catholicae* Lib. III, c. 6, n. 2; also see R. Schwarz p. 434.

19. See R. Schwarz p. 436; J. J. Cuneo 'The Power of Jurisdiction: Empowerment for Church Functioning and Mission Distinct from the Power of Orders', in J. H. Provost ed., *The Church as Mission* (Washington, D.C.: Canon Law Society of America 1984) p. 190.

20. See R. Schwarz p. 439.

21. See F. Suarez *Commentaria ac disputationes in tertiam partem D. Thomae*, q. 8, a. 6, in L. Vives, ed. *Opera omnia* Vol. XVII (Paris 1960) p. 646.

22. See F. X. Wernz p. 13.

23. See R. Schwarz p. 441.

24. See K. Mörsdorf 'De sacra potestate' *Apollonaris* 40 (1967) 45–46; B. Kloppenburg *The Ecclesiology of Vatican II* trans. M. J. O'Connell (Chicago, Illinois: Franciscan Herald Press, 1974) (from the original Portuguese: *A Eclesiologia do Vaticano II*, Rio de Janeiro 1971), pp. 124–166; V. de Paolis, 'De natura sacramentali potestatis sacrae', *Periodica* 65 (1976) 68–72; U. Navarrete, pp. 471–472; R. Schwarz, pp. 443–444.

25. See *AAS* 57 (1965) 11. Translation from A. P. Flannery ed., *Documents of Vatican II* (Grand Rapids, Michigan: Eerdmans, 1975), p. 357.

26. See *LG*, 20, *AAS* 57 (1965) 23; *Presbuterorum ordinis* (= *PO*), 2, *AAS* 58 (1966) 992.

27. See U. Navarrete p. 472.

28. See K. Mörsdorf pp. 42–42; J. B. Beyer 'De natura potestatis regiminis seu iurisdictionis recte in codice renovato enuntianda', *Periodica* 71 (1982) 104–106; U. Navarrete, pp. 472–475.

29. See *PO*, 2, *AAS* 58 (1966) 992.

30. See *Optatam totius*, 9, *AAS* 58 (1966) 719.

31. See *Gaudium et spes*, 76, *AAS* 58 (1966) 1099; see also R. Schwarz p. 442; *Dignitatis humanae*, 2–4, *AAS* 58 (1966) 930–933; P. Pavan 'Declaration on Religious Freedom', in H. Vorgrimler, ed. *Commentary on the Documents of Vatican II*, Vol. IV (Freiburg 1969), pp. 53–72.

32. See P. Sieghart *The Lawful Rights of Mankind: An Introduction to the International Legal Code of Human Rights* (Oxford 1986), pp. 170–237.

33. See X. Ochoa *Index verborum ac locutionum codicis iuris canonici* (Roma 1983), pp. 355–356, 462–463.

34. See G. Michiels *De potestate ordinaria et delegata* (Parisii 1964), p. 133; V. de Paolis 'De significatione verborum iurisdictio "ordinaria", "delegata", "mandata", "vicaria" ', *Periodica* 54 (1965) 510–512, 515–516; U. Navarrete p. 480.

35. Cf. U. Navarrete p. 480.

Patrick Granfield

Legitimation and Bureaucratisation of Ecclesial Power

QUESTIONS OF legitimation and bureaucratisation emerge in every complex social unit. These two components have considerable impact on the stability and vitality of institutions and can foster or impede their effectiveness. The Catholic Church is no exception, possessing as it does recognised structures of authority, a bureaucratic organisation, common goals, and doctrinal and disciplinary beliefs uniting its eight hundred and sixty-six million adherents.

1. THE MEANING OF LEGITIMATION

In reference to the Roman Catholic Church, it is helpful to distinguish legitimacy and legitimation. Most of the literature deals with civil societies where power comes directly from the people. Legitimacy, therefore, describes authority as valid, and legitimation, the process by which this validity is justified. On-going concern in civil society focuses on both the existence and exercise of authority. In the Church, however, the transmission theory of power does not apply: leaders are designated by people, but their power comes directly from God and not from the people. Pope and bishops, appointed according to the proper procedures, are legitimate. Disputes are usually not over the existence of authority but its exercise.

By *legitimacy* in an ecclesial context, I mean that power which is established in accord with the law, divine and positive. Legitimacy refers to the possession of ecclesial power. It is *de jure* or objective authority. One has it or one does not; it is a factual either/or. The authority of duly appointed and ordained

Pope and bishops, as long as they remain in the faith, is legitimate; it is power that has its source in God (Rom. 13:1) and shares in the authority of Christ through the Holy Spirit.

By *legitimation*, I mean the acceptance of the exercise of authority by the members of the Church. Do the faithful find ecclesial authority credible, have confidence in it, and follow its directions? Legitimation, as a justification of the exercise of authority, refers to *de facto* or subjective reception and efficacy of authority. It is a matter of degree, more or less present. Therefore we speak of a crisis of legitimation in the Church rather than a crisis of legitimacy.

Legitimation is a response to authority; it is complete when the goals of the member and the goals of the institution coincide. Accordingly, S. M. Lipset speaks of 'the capacity of the system to engender and maintain the belief that the existing institutions are the most appropriate ones for the society.[1] Those in authority must act (and be seen to act) in harmony with the norms that are valued in that particular society.[2]

Because the Church is a voluntary organisation, there is a greater need for legitimation. A high level of legitimation is accorded to the institutions of Church, when the faithful approve of their actions and consider them credible and authentic. Confidence in Church authority is a fragile entity and is easier to lose than to restore. Legitimation is a fluctuating measure of consensus; it has ebbed and flowed throughout the history of the Church.

Max Weber in his analysis of dominion—the probability that the commands of those in authority will be obeyed—noted that people obey for a variety of reasons.[3] Habit, intellectual convictions, and affective motivations may influence obedience, but they do not of themselves establish stable authority. What is needed is belief in the legitimacy of authority—the conviction that the authority figure has the right to command and that the subjects have the corresponding duty to obey.

In analysing the grounds for establishing legitimacy, Weber proposed three principal types: legal, traditional, and charismatic. This three-fold division is applicable to our topic of the legitimation of ecclesial power.

First, the *legal type* of legitimacy rests on the belief that the power of the ruler is grounded in law. Thus bishops in the Church through valid appointment and ordination receive from Christ according to divine law their power to act as pastors of the Christian community. The Code of Canon Law explains in detail the legal character of ecclesial authority. Besides specific canons on the Pope, bishops, cardinals, and other officials, it also delineates the nature of juridic acts (Cans. 124–128), the power of governance (Cans. 129–144), and the meaning of ecclesiastical offices (Cans. 145–196). The latter section also deals with the conferral of office and its loss by resignation, transfer, removal, or privation.

The legal basis of legitimacy is framed according to a monarchial understanding of Church authority; it remains a problem for those who live in a democracy. Many Catholics question the primatial claims of unelected officials and advocate a greater role for the clergy and laity in the selection of bishops.

Second, the *traditional type* of legitimacy rests on reverence for tradition. This upholds the legitimacy and fosters the credibility of those office holders who are appointed as heirs of a long-standing and revered tradition. A good example is the conviction that bishops are the successors of the apostles, and the Pope, the successor of Peter and Vicar of Christ. The Catholic Church relies on scripture and tradition, including in the latter conciliar and dogmatic teachings. Fidelity to the past helps the Church preserve continuity, yet it may make modern adaptations and creative change difficult. The traditional basis also becomes less convincing in a complex world of accelerated change and pluralistic views, where an appeal to unchanging traditions appears to some anachronistic.

Third, the *charismatic type* of legitimacy rests on the power of extraordinary holiness, heroism, and intellectual or political brilliance, augmented by the aura of the office. Although there are advantages to genuine charismatic authority, it can become disproportionate, as exemplified by the cult of the papacy in the nineteenth and early twentieth centuries. Catholic tradition has from antiquity insisted on the distinction between the office and the person. Augustine and others responded to the Donatist heresy by arguing that unworthy ministers can still perform valid sacramental acts. So the charismatic dimension is a help but not a necessity.

Church authority is objectively legitimate, but it still has to be subjectively appropriated by the faithful. Failure to accept the authority of the Church may not affect its essential core, but it certainly renders it less efficacious and effective. A vital, believing community needs members who have confidence in its God-given authority and are willing to support it.

2. THE CRISIS OF LEGITIMATION

A crisis of legitimation occurs when there is a serious conflict between the goals of the institution and the demands of the members. Such conflicts, rightly or wrongly arrived at, can result in a loss of confidence and credibility in the institution. To some degree there is always tension between authority and autonomy: it becomes a crisis when the tension becomes so exacerbated that social harmony is severely affected.

I have examined this problem elsewhere in terms of systems analysis.[4] Briefly, Church authority operates through a system of operations: symbolic actions (communication of faith, morals, values, and policies); distributions (spiritual, social, educational benefits); rules (both disciplinary and doctrinal); and extractions (requests for financial support and personal services). Members of the Church respond to these four categories through supports or demands. They may support these four categories by their respect, participation, obedience, and generosity, or they may formulate demands that reflect their discontent, frustration, and hunger for power, equality, or other values.

In the Church today an increase in demands and a resistance to supports has created a crisis of legitimation or credibility. Let us examine the kind of concrete circumstances that have occasioned this crisis.

First, demands that run counter to the traditional goals and basic tenets of an organisation tend to undermine its exercise of power. Some Catholics oppose the Church's teaching on sexual morality, mandatory celibacy for priests, the mission of the laity, and the role of women. 'Selective or *à la carte* Catholicism' is a growing phenomenon. Many Catholics, following only those teachings of the Church that they agree with, still consider themselves good and loyal members.

The response of Roman authorities, especially under the pontificate of John Paul II, has been to look with suspicion on the pluralism and free-ranging theological debates of the post-conciliar era. Seeking to present an unambiguous Catholic identity, the Pope and the curial congregations strongly affirm traditional teachings, censure theologians and others who would depart from them, and repudiate any innovations they view as dangerous. The issue of dissent from non-infallible teaching continues to be a source of division that affects legitimation.

Second, changes within the institution can also influence legitimation. The reform of traditional institutions and the establishment of new ones often create an unsettling atmosphere. Ideological and structural problems have arisen in such areas as the implementation of collegiality, the renewal of clerical and religious life, the liturgical reform, the development of the role of the laity, and the ecumenical dialogue. In periods of transition the institution has the difficult task of protecting the value of continuity as a source of legitimation as it attempts to respond to urgent pastoral needs.

Third, the crisis of legitimation may also be linked to organised groups who challenge the exercise of Church authority. Special interest groups—such as those that focus on abortion, women's rights, and homosexuality—form a mixed coalition of organised opposition to the Church's teaching. Excessive and prolonged division within the Church can harm legitimation. The Church cannot be expected to abdicate its authority; yet what it sees as fidelity to tradition is often seen by others as reactionary intransigence.

There is no single response to the multi-causal crisis of legitimation, as the Church tries to balance acceptable conflict and desired consensus. Resolving critical issues before new ones arise is important, since delays in resoultion may encourage extreme positions. The Church cannot compromise what it holds as part of its essential tradition, but neither should it refuse to acknowledge that changes in some Church teachings are possible in light of historical research and of cultural and intellectual developments.

A participatory, 'dialogical', and expressive style of communication can do much to alleviate crises of legitimation, for example, by increasing the number of channels through which a wide number of individuals would be involved in the decision-making process. The consultations, hearings, and interviews that were conducted in the preparation for the pastoral letters of the US bishops on war and peace and on the American economy furnish a good example of a workable process.

3. THE MEANING OF BUREAUCRACY

Max Weber suggested that bureaucracy is the most efficient form of human organisation. Although that view has been disputed, the fact remains that bureaucracy is pervasive in nearly all social groups. It is especially evident in governments, businesses, educational and charitable institutions, and churches.

In one sense, bureaucracy has a positive connotation. It is a managerial device used by large organisations to organise their activities and to accomplish their set goals. A bureaucracy, then, is a body of non-elected officials—a professional and permanent staff—who function as administrators. If an institution can be defined as a pattern of practices for the shaping and sharing of values, then a bureacracy forms a kind of sub-institution responsible for administration. The bureaucrats are in charge of various bureaux, agencies, or offices where the daily adminstration of policy takes place. Elected officials may come and go, but the bureaucracy remains to assure a smooth transition of power and the continuence of the system.

Ideally, then, bureaucracy is seen as a desirable principle of organisation. When a system becomes too large for one person to administer it and division of labour is a necessity, then some forms of bureaucracy is almost inevitable. The bureaucrats or civil servants form a devoted core of skilled professionals who keep the system working, contribute to its stability, and promote its legitimation. Those who extoll the value of bureaucracy mention the virtues of the professional civil servant: efficiency, industry, integrity, impartiality, courtesy, and responsiveness.

Nonetheless, bureaucracy often has a negative meaning. It is described pejoratively as a system of administration marked by red tape, proliferation, rigidity, narrowness, waste, and favouritism. In contrast to the admirable qualities of the bureaucrats given above, a prevailing view characterises these officials as inefficient, impersonal, arrogant, manipulative, and venal. Bureaucracy is sometimes called the disease of large organisations because of its resistance to change and fear of innovation. Bureaucracies can encourage inefficiency because they tend to grow in size. Parkinson's law puts it neatly: 'Work expands so as to fill the time available for its completion.' Other criticism focuses on the conflict between bureaucracy and the democratic values of openness, individual freedom, protection of rights, and due process.

If some forms bureaucracy become an illness in large corporate bodies, then how is it cured? Social scientists make several suggestions: the right to criticise, improved management techniques, more effective training and selection of officials, procedures than ensure fair decision-making, openness, better relationships with the public, and elimination of excessive delays, paper work, and red tape.

4. THE BUREAUCRATISATION OF THE CHURCH

The creation of multiple offices and staffs arises from the desire to provide effective administration and service for a sizeable membership. In the United States, for example, ecclesiastical bureaucracy in all communions has grown proportionately faster than the growth of the membership. Between 1900 and the present the number of Catholic dioceses in the United States has grown by nearly eighty per cent.

The increasing bureaucratisation is even more striking when one considers the recent development of new diocesan, national, and international agencies that were not in existence in 1900. An interesting exercise is to consult the US Catholic Directory and compare the description of any American Catholic diocese in 1960 with its description in 1988. One fact clearly emerges: there has been a veritable bureaucratic explosion in the size of the organisation and in the number of offices and staff. Diocesan chanceries today are complex structural organisations housed in large buildings with numerous offices, paid professional employees, computerised equipment, and a budget of several million dollars.

In the Church's central administration similar bureaucratisation has occurred and with it the need for updating. In fact, the Curia has been reformed several times, most significantly by Pius X and Paul VI. The Fathers of Vatican II and the first Extraordinary Synod in 1969 called for curial reform. In 1983, a commission of cardinals was appointed to study reform measures, and a year later prepared a schema. It was discussed at the meeting of the cardinals in November 1985. James Provost in his analysis of this schema discussed several critical issues: secret procedures, overlapping competencies, conflicting responses, and the lack of any established system for recruiting, training, and evaluating curial personnel.[5] He also called for greater clarity regarding the relationship between the college of cardinals, the Roman Curia, and the synod of bishops.

The increased bureaucratisation at both the diocesan, national, and international levels raises several theological and practical questions. From a theological viewpoint bureaucratic organisation should not devolve into a monolithic or unilateral exercise of authority that would bypass the rights and responsibilities of members of the local churches. The ecclesiology of communion, supported by both Vatican II and the 1985 Synod, affirmed that the universal Church is not primarily a juridical entity but fundamentally the communion of local churches, each of which is truly Church. The principles of collegiality, subsidiarity, and legitimate diversity should be reflected in the administrative life of the universal Church. The Bishop of Rome has the special ministry to promote and protect the unity of the whole Church. The Roman Curia assits him and is in frequent contact with the local churches.[6]

On a practical level, the bureaucratic system of the Church diminishes its legitimation when it neglects consultation, collaboration, accountability, and due process and when it assumes an adversarial and negative attitude. A overly monarchical and centralised bureaucracy distances itself from the faithful and loses its contract with urgent pastoral needs. Administrative procedures and management styles have to be critically assessed, in order to avoid the undesirable aspects of bureaucracy such as inflexibility, cumbersomeness, inefficiency, and unfairness.

Ecclesiastical bureaucracy is not an end in itself but is always at the service of the kingdom. When it respects the freedom of the believers and is inspired by the Gospel imperative of love, it can enhance the legitimation of ecclesial authority and elicit deep devotion and commitment. The words of Vatican II are worth recalling: 'Those ministers who are endowed with sacred power are servants of their brethren, so that all who are of the People of God, and therefore enjoy a true Christian dignity, can work toward a common goal freely and in an orderly way, and arrive at salvation' (LG 18).

Notes

1. S. M. Lipset *Political Man* (New York 1963) 64.

2. See F. X. Kaufmann 'The Sociology of Knowledge and the Problem of Authority', *Journal of Ecumenical Studies* 19 (1982) 18–31, and *Kirche begreifen. Analysen und Thesen zur gesellschaftlichen Verfassung des Christentums* (Freiburg 1979).

3. See M. Weber *Wirtschaft und Gesellschaft. Grundriss der verstehenden Soziologie*, 4th ed. (Tübingen 1956). English translation, *Economy and Society*, eds. G. Ross and C. Wittich, translated by E. Fischoff et al. (Berkely 1978).

4. P. Granfield *Ecclesial Cybernetics: A Study of Democracy in the Church* (New York 1973).

5. See J. Provost 'Reform of the Roman Curia' in G. Albergio and J. Provost, eds., *Synod 1985—An Evaluation*, Concilium, No. 188 (Edinburgh 1986) 26–36.

6. For a fuller treatment of these themes see P. Granfield *The Limits of the Papacy: Authority and Autonomy in the Church* (New York 1987).

Patrick Valdrini

The Exercise of Power and the Principle of Submission

THE LATIN Code of canon law does not set out a general theory of the power of ecclesiastical government and does not specifically tackle the problems of how to apply the principle of submission of people to the decisions which affect them. On the other hand, it makes rules for the exercise of ecclesiastical power. Does it acknowledge that it is possible for the faithful not to submit to the decisions of those who exercise this power? Failure to submit to a decision creates an opposition or, rather, a conflict, and that is why the answer to this question depends on an analysis, in the codified legal text, of the procedures which allow the faithful to appeal against acts of authority. Do such procedures exist in the Code? An affirmative reply would show that canon law acknowledges that people have the right to assert their opinions and arguments and not to be forced to submit without discussion or examination.

1. JURIDICAL ACTS AND SUBMISSION

Juridical acts are the expression of the exercise of ecclesiastical governmental power, traditionally distinguished as legislative power, judiciary power, and executive or administrative power. In legislative power, these acts are the ecclesiastical laws, in judiciary power they are the sentences, and in executive power they are the decisions or administrative acts. A holder of government power has the right to demand the submission of others having shown his intention in the required legal form. This form depends on the rules of existence of every juridical act and on the legally defined conditions which

94

concern each act in particular.[1] Taking account of this legitimacy clause, one *submits to* a law, to a sentence, or to an administrative decision.

The need to demand the required legal form rests on two motives. Firstly, before the acquisition of this form an act is in a phase of preparation or development. This phase allows those who are going to take a decision to assemble the necessary elements for this decision taking. Secondly, to be effective the act must be brought to the attention of the people. For the law, a promulgation is necessary, for a sentence, a publication, and for an administrative act, a notification. This requirement is of great importance, as much from the point of view of the exercise of power as of the obligation to submit which goes with it. The publication of the decision corresponds to a commitment by the authority which thereby defines its will, most often in writing and, for certain acts, with a detailed reasoning. The authority imposes a judgment on the action and requires submission.

2. SUBMISSION TO LAWS

Canon law is binding by the will of the legislator.[2] The Code makes no mention of an obligation depending on the acceptance of the law by those who have to enforce it.[3] The conditions of obligation concern the competence of the legislator or of the legislative instrument and even the content of the law in a case when the law is carried by a lower-ranking legislator.[4] No ruling is given in the Code concerning the content of universal laws.[5] On the other hand the respect for higher law is directly guaranteed in the case of legislative activity at Bishops conferences and special councils. Before being promulgated, new laws must be 'recognised' by the Holy See.[6] This 'recognition' is a sort of stamp of agreement indicating that the content of the law comes within the framework of universal law. It is the task of the supreme legislator. As for laws issuing from a diocesan bishop, even carried after consultations or on the occasion of a synod, they take their legal force from their promulgation by the bishop, sole legislator.[7]

Submission to the law is not demanded from the moment of its promulgation. Provision is made for a delay in application, called *vacatio legis*. Except in special cases defined by the legislator himself, the delay is three months for universal laws and one month for particular laws. This delay is generally explained as a time for taking account of the new arrangements by interested parties and of preparation for bringing new regulations into force. With the promulgation the time of drawing up the law is finished and the passing of the period of delay legally allowed before the application of the law corresponds to the moment when submission is required.

Is there any possibility of appeal against the application of a law? Indeed, reasons concerning the appropriateness of its promulgation or concerning its content can justify requests for the deferment of the delay in application period, for modification or even for abrogation of the law.

The Code does not allow for any appeal against the laws and, to the best of our knowledge, no legal text mentions it.[8] Canonic doctrine, however, allows that the faithful can approach the writer of a law to let him know their opinion. Also mentioned is the unanimity of the authors to allow for bishops, individually or collectively, to make an appeal to the Holy See against laws which have universal significance.[9]

The problem arises from the fact that doctrinal solutions are not legally recognised. In that way the appeals mentioned are *praeter legem*/'beside the law' like the submission for a legal decision (*recours gracieux*) which, under the system of the old Code, people could bring before the diocesan bishops in the case of decisions prejudicial to them. Today this submission has become part of the Code and has found a binding juridical form.[10] The same does not apply for appeals against the laws.[11] Also unanswered are questions of real importance: which laws can be the subject of appeal? Who can make an appeal and under what conditions? In the case of prejudice could one benefit from a suspensive appeal? What delays should be applicable? Who should know about such appeals?

The plan for the promulgation of a basic law at the time of the revision of the Code of canon law had started the process of introducing a form of control over the constitutionality of the laws in the Church. The drawing up of such a law in fact posed the problem of the hierarchy of ecclesiastical norms. Some suggestions had been made which gave the faithful the opportunity to have stated, at the very highest level, the way in which certain laws failed to conform with the basic principles regulating institutions and personal status.[12] The abandonment of this plan effectively left the problem untreated, the actual text of the Code, as we said earlier, containing no further indications on the matter.

Without denying that the questions raised by the establishment of appeals procedures go beyond the procedural order itself and concern just as much the nature of ecclesiastical power as the actual conditions of its exercise, the fact of having a mere practical recognition of these appeals is harmful. It tends to give substance to the idea that the exercise of legislative power is not subject to any control in the Church. At all events, it helps to develop the feeling that the only attitude looked for in the Church is one of submission.[13] The majority of state-controlled systems are in fact currently seeking to extend the means of controlling the activity of legislators.

In practice, given the state of the legislation, it is necessary to take greater account of the principle of public opinion in the Church. We know the recognition it receives from specialists in state-controlled constitutional law who consider it as a control over the legislative action of governments. The canonic legislator already grants it a place by recognising that the faithful, according to the knowledge, ability and prestige which they enjoy, have the right and the duty to give their opinion to the holy pastors on anything which affects the good of the Church.[14] This place should be extended and given a juridical form.

3. SUBMISSION TO JUDICIAL SENTENCES

In the matter of appeal against judicial sentences, the law offers elaborate legislation.[15] Civil or penal, declaratory or constituent, the sentences are always subject to possible action by interested parties. There are many grounds for this. They may concern the juridical elements on which the sentence is based (competence of the judge, refusal of the right of defence ...), or the injustice of the content. The legal institutions at people's disposal are well known: they are a plea of nullity and an appeal to a higher judge, with time limits in each case which prevent the actions from pending indefinitely.

Submission to the judicial sentence is demanded at the moment when the action passes to the state of judgment. This measure concerns social order. From that point an objection to the decision becomes impossible, except in the case of manifest injustice which would have to be established by a court of law and which could result in the action being reinstated at the point at which it was brought before a judge.[16] Finally, in cases which concern personal status (marriage, ordination ...), submission to the decision of the judge is not irreversible. New evidence or serious new arguments would justify the request for a re-examination of the case.

4. SUBMISSION TO ADMINISTRATIVE DECISIONS

In relation to the previous code, revised canonic legislation has developed the parts of the law devoted to the exercise of administrative power. This power consists of the application of the laws. This important activity is carried out by the organisations of the Holy See which enjoy a governmental power but also, according to the extent of their competence, by the vicars general and episcopal vicars, the principal superiors of clerical Institutes of consecrated life as well as those to whom authority has been delegated. The exercise of this power gives rise to general and particular administrative acts. The first clarify for a group of people the mode of enforcement of the law or in urgent cases the observation of the law (general executory decrees and instructions). The second contain decisions intended for particular individuals. These decisions are usually defined as manifestations of the will of the executive authority, in particular cases, with the aim of imposing a judgment on the action of individuals (decrees and precepts)[17] or to answer a request made by an individual (rescript containing a dispensation, a privilege or other grace).[18]

It is appeals against these particular administrative acts which, over the past few years, have received significant legal recognition. In fact, the 1983 Code goes back to a system laid down by the previous Code and perfected by Paul VI in 1967—giving it a better juridical form. Today, a person having cause to complain of a decision affecting him could set in motion a system of inspection of the form and content of the decision. This system begins by a request to the legislator to modify or withdraw it.[19] It continues—if this is necessary—with an appeal to the hierarchical authority and, if the final decision taken emanates from a Congregation of the Roman Curia,[20] it brings the parties before an administrative tribunal, the second department of the Apostolic Segnatura, created at the time of the reform of the Roman Curia in 1967.[21]

Canonists know the debates which the establishment of this system has provoked. The majority agree in recognising the great advance represented by the introduction of a juridical examination of the complaints of injured parties. But problems still remain over which the debate continues.[22] One of the most important concerns the increase in the number of administrative tribunals. In effect the Apostolic Segnatura is the only tribunal for the whole Church. This situation is dissuasive. It explains why so few appeals reach this court, a fact which is due not to the lack of contentious matters within the Church but to the inconvenience represented by the necessity to bring one's appeal before the supreme tribunal.[23]

In addition, the obligation to pass through a chain of administrative appeals (to the legislator then to his hierarchical superior) before reaching the legal proceedings helps to make the tribunal difficult of access. One can well imagine that the complainants find more security in the examination of the appeal conducted according to a binding legal procedure, with the assurance of hearing a judge pronounce a sentence which is imposed on each party. In fact, this compulsory procedure for examining an appeal before the holders of executive power, particularly the hierarchical superior, corresponds to the desire of canon law to prevent claims from becoming too easily contentious.

The law in fact increases its appeals for conciliation and mediation.[24] So for this type of conflict, the Conference of bishops, or each bishop if the Conference does not do it, can create an office of mediator or a council of mediation composed of particularly competent people, with the aim of helping to find solutions to the conflicts which bring people into opposition with each other.[25] In spite of the publicity surrounding this canon, in France, for example, this recommendation is not in fact followed. One may wonder whether this indifference does not arise from an unwillingness to become involved. The very idea of conciliation, often advanced in cases of conflict is readily under suspicion by reason of the link which is made with a possible application of the principle of submission.

In reality, the risk is not attached to conciliation itself, nor to mediation. On the one hand an attempt at conciliation never ends with a binding sentence, the people empowered to exercise this function proposing solutions which the parties are free to accept or reject. On the other hand, conciliation does not take place without the observation of procedural rules defined in statutes or at the time of the constitution of an office. In truth, the poor reception which these terms attract comes rather from a fear nourished by an inflationary use of the principle of communion in the Church. The legitimate wish to avoid matters of dispute does not make legal appeals superfluous. Canonists must show that the existence of elaborate appeal procedures does not conflict with the principle of communion and that it is the guarantee of an extension of the principle of respectful submission and the rights of individuals.

Finally we ask if it is possible to appeal in this way against general executory decrees or instructions. The answer is negative, for the system described above only concerns appeals against particular administrative acts. Appeals against general administrative acts have the character of a submission for a legal decision *praeter legem* (*recours gracieux*) and, let us repeat, they do not receive an elaborated form from the law. Against administrative acts of this nature emanating from a Congregation of the Roman Curia, people have at their disposal 'the benefit of a new hearing' mentioned in the general Regulation of the Curia[27] but in connection with which no written procedure exists. Against the general administrative acts of other holders of executive power, it is allowed that an appeal to the superior of the act is possible. But there again, no procedure exists.

The code specifies however that the content of these general acts may not be contrary to the laws if it wishes to have any legal value,[28] a legitimate recognition in our particular field because of the submission of administrative acts to the laws which they enforce. So not only must the lack of clearly defined procedures be exposed, but also the absence of a jurisdictional appeal like the one which is established for the examination of complaints against particular administrative acts. Jurists certainly know what difficult questions are raised by the examination of the legal relationship of general administrative acts (regulations, circulars) to the laws, as shown by past and present developments of state-controlled administrative procedures. They also recognise the importance of jurisprudence in order to guarantee the correct exercise of administrative power.[29]

Our presentation has shown that canon law ought still to progress towards the creation of institutions which indicate clearly that the exercise of ecclesiastical power cannot be arbitrary.[30] The just application of the principle of submission in the Church is not merely tied to the definition of the terms of existence of juridical acts. It depends on the establishment of genuine appeal procedures allowing the faithful to oppose acts of power, within the framework of the law. Without these appeals, and without procedures which give them a clearly elaborated juridical form, the application of the principle of submission risks becoming more widespread according to the influences which shape it. In such an undertaking, canon law and the Church, with their conception of the exercise of power, put their credibility at stake.

Translated by Barrie Mackay

Notes

1. These rules concern the capacity of the person who performs the act, his freedom, and then the act itself which should combine 'the constituent elements which are essential to it.' (can. 124 § 1), and finally the respect for the formalities imposed by the law on pain of nullity (as, for example, the necessary consultation of a council).

2. Can. 7: the law is established when it is promulgated.

3. Can. 7 quotes the first part of a text from Gratien's Decree (D. 4, dpc 3) and leaves aside the second part: ... *firmantur cum moribus intentium approbantur*/'they (the laws) are confirmed when they are approved by those who apply them.'

4. In fact can. 135 § 2 says that 'a law contrary to higher law cannot validly be brought in by a lower-ranking legislator.'

5. This is the task of doctrine. It is found widely set out in works which concern the code of 1917. For example, G. Michiels *Normae generales juris canonici* (Rome 1949), vol. 1 pp. 152–192. The supreme legislative power is exercised by the Roman Pontiff and by the college of bishops in union with the Pope. This power, which can judge the extent of its own competence, is limited by the observation of the prescriptions of divine law. However can. 333 § 2 declares that in the exercise of his charge the Roman Pontiff is bound in communion with the other bishops and with the whole Church.

6. Cann. 446 and 455 § 2. The *recognitio*/'recognition' is a specifically canonic term.

7. Can. 466: 'In the diocesan synod, the diocesan bishop is the only legislator ...'

8. Perhaps, but only for particular cases, the mechanism of the dispensation without just or reasonable cause, reserved for the legislator himself or his superior because this case directly concerns the law, might be a means of recognising the non-application of the law. See Can. 90 § 1: There is no dispensation from an ecclesiastical law without just and reasonable cause, taking account of the circumstances, the case, and the importance of the law which is the subject of dispensation; otherwise the

dispensation is illicit and, unless given by the legislator or his superior, it is invalid.

9. See Ch. Lefèbvre, art. 'Lois ecclésiastiques' in *Dict. de droit canonique*, t. 6, col. 645.

10. See below, note 19.

11. One is confronted by forms of 'unorganised juridical sanctions' as defined, for the activity of state-controlled legislators, by G. Burdeau *Traité de science politique*, t. 4, *le statut du pouvoir dans l'Etat*, (Paris L.G.D.J.), pp. 451–534.

12. See P. Lombardia, J. Hervada, J. A. Souto 'Sugerencias para la revision del proyecto' in *El proyecto de ley fundamental de la Iglesia. Texto y analisis critico*, (Pamplona, Ed. universidad de Navarra 1971), pp. 218–226. See in the same work, the article of J. A. Souto 'Jerarquia personal y organizacion', *ibid.* pp. 173–179.

13. It would of course be necessary to complete this analysis by research into participation in the formulation of laws in the Church.

14. Can. 212 § 3.

15. Although no canon treats appeals against laws, a whole title—21 canons— (cann. 1619–1640) is devoted to methods of bringing action against a sentence.

16. Can. 1645–1648.

17. Can. 48–58.

18. Can. 59–93.

19. This request which is granted a procedure (can. 1734) was in the old Code a submission for a legal decision *praeter legem* (*recours gracieux*).

20. The system could begin with a decision of the Roman Congregation.

21. Cann. 1732–1739 and 1445 § 2.

22. See our work *Injustices et protection des droits dans l'Eglise* (Strasbourg, Cerdic-publications 1983), p. 426. See also among the most recent publications: K. Matthews 'The development and future of the administrative tribunal' in *Studia canonica* 18, 1984, p. 233 and J. Schlick 'Des limites de la justice administrative dans l'Eglise catholique' in *Praxis juridique et religion*, 3, 1986, pp. 127–135.

23. The schemas of the present code proposed the creation of administrative tribunals by the Conferences of bishops.

24. Thus can. 1446 § 1: All the faithful, and especially the bishops, will do their utmost, with respect for doctrine, to avoid disputes among God's people, and to settle them quickly in a peaceful manner.

25. Can. 1733.

26. See our note, 'La résolution juridique des conflits dans l'Eglise', in *Documents episcopats*, 17, 1986, p 5.

27. *Act. Apost. Sedis*, 60, 1968, p. 166, art. 119.

28. Cann. 33 § 1 and 34 § 2.

29. See our note 'Le manque de jurisprudence administrative canonique' in *Le supplément* 155, 1985, pp. 129–131.

30. See principles no. 6 and 7 of the Principles of revision of the Code of canon law voted in the synod of bishops of 1967: 'Principia quae Codicis Iuris Canonici recognitionem dirigant', in *Communicationes*, 2, 1969, pp. 82–84.

PART III

PART III

Joseph Comblin

The Power of the Church and the Powers of Evil: the Case of Latin America

RECENT EVENTS, particularly in the Middle East, have recalled that the world religions—notably Islam but not only Islam—can play an important role within societies on the political plane and even on the military. Today's world is far from being entirely secularised. Religion is still powerful. It can still make society submit; it can still shape and direct it. Historical phenomena like *Christianity and the crusades* have still their equivalents in our time. But it is not that particular aspect of religious power that we are going to look at here.

Elsewhere—in Latin America—we hear a good deal of talk about the influence which the Church can, or could, exercise on the development of peoples, indeed on needful revolution. On the left the famous phrase of Che Guevara is not forgotten—the phrase in which he proclaimed that revolution in Latin America would be invincible the day the Christians took responsibility for it. Many writers compute the historical potentialities of the Church and the chances it has of playing a decisive political role on that continent. In this way the power of the Church, of Christianity and of Christians, is looked at in terms that are purely political and sociological.

One may indeed look at the question of the Church's power from a purely political angle or, if preferred, in a sense that is purely technical or operational. If we hold to the political or sociological perspective, there is the risk of understanding the action of the Church in the world—this action which is so charged with power—in a way that is totally pragmatic. The Church makes use of power for its own safety or its own expansion; in other words, to affirm its own grandeur. Given our history, we are far from denying that this has often played an important role which, still today, can explain many procedures in terms of this political pragmatism. The Church also does behave like a political party or a lobby, even if in theory it claims freedom from such distortions.

Alongside what cannot be denied, there is nevertheless another reality, another form of power or authority of the Church, and which has a directly theological sense, for it has its source in the work of Christ himself.

1. THE POWER OF THE CHURCH IN THE SERVICE OF THE POOR

What we are witnessing in Latin America is the power of the Church against the forces of evil. The location of the power of the Church is not in its internal life but in its action in the world. The gospels show us Jesus in combat with demons. St Paul shows us the risen Jesus triumphant over the powers that dominate the world. Christ has handed on this power to his Church. That is what is happening in Latin America. Political action by isolated individuals and official persons on their own individual responsibility far from exhausts the account of Christian action. On the contrary it is the Church itself, collectively—as an entity that places all its weight in the balance—that brings into play the power that it has on global society. For the Church has weight—influence—on global society: on the State and on the whole gamut of institutions of civil authority. The Church enters the struggle in defence of, and for the liberation of, the poor and the oppressed. It enters the fight as an entity entirely committed, even if a certain number of Catholics do not agree. In the eyes of society it is the Church which is committed: in Latin America that is quite clear. The Church acts through the intermediary of certain institutions with which public opinion identifies it: the *Vicariat de la Solidarité* in Santiago in Chile, the Justice and Peace Commissions in Brazil, the *Commission pour la pastorale de la terre*, the CIMI for the defence of the Indians, the movement of the landless, etc. In other countries these institutions are more localised, but *at the level of the local Church they represent the Church*, for example at Riobamba in Equador, in the region of the southern Andes in Peru, and in the diocese of San Salvador in El Salvador.

The power of the Church is not found here in the service of a party or class, it does not aim at the conquest of power for itself or for its allies. The Church wills a radical change in society, a total liberation of the world.

The power of the Church sets itself against the system of National Security taken as a whole. It does not will the destruction of human beings, but rather a global system of social life.

Puebla offers a first theological approach to this fight in speaking of the struggle against the new idolatry: of absolute political power, money (see Puebla 405, 491,493 & 500). Consequently the Church does not struggle simply against social factors—human forces. It struggles against forces of evil, forces that are beyond simple sociological factors—forces where evil is incarnated in a mode which the Bible calls 'the demons'.

The battle for the liberation of the poor (Puebla 1134) is a confrontation between two more than terrestrial powers: the power of Christ and the power of the demons. Thus it is more than a straight political battle in the technical or secularised sense of the word.

This battle produces severe internal tensions in the bosom of the Church. Many do not accept it (Puebla 1139). Even so the latin-american Church assembled at Medellin and at Puebla assesses this struggle as corresponding to its mission. Such a struggle leads to conflict with social groups and with individuals, notably with the structures of power and with their spokesmen. Medellin and Puebla consider that *conflicts like this are necessary* (Puebla 1138). This same battle comes down from the level of moral principles to the plane of concrete cases where it calls into question *very concrete situations* (Puebla 1138).

The power of the Church produces effects: Haiti, the Philippines, South Korea—but also to some extent Brazil, Peru, San Salvador, Nicaragua—are proof of this. Moreover the poor call on the power of the Church. They see it as their last refuge and their last protection. Despite so many occasions of disillusion which for them smack of betrayal, the poor have found support enough still to believe that for them the Church is the presence of the power of Christ on earth. It does not seem to them possible that the risen Christ remains totally powerless, and that he shows no signs of his power.

2. THE POWER OF THE BISHOPS

The Power of the Church is incarnate in the power of the bishop. In Latin America we have rediscovered the power of the bishop. When the bishop lacks strength or courage—or indeed simply lacks intuition—the whole Church is crippled and cannot act on society: it remains without effect in the face of the idols: look at Argentina or Colombia. On the other hand when the bishop—or still better, the bishops' conference—incarnates the witness of its people and places itself at the side of the poor, it *takes on power*. It often takes time to exhaust the resistance of the enemy. But the enemy does fall back and does weaken. If in Brazil or Chile the bishops had been silent as in Argentina, the number of victims of oppression would have been much greater. In Argentina the silence of the bishops must indirectly have caused the death of thousands of additional victims.

What is worth while is first of all the *presence of the bishop* on the field of battle: on the land stolen by the great, in the work place, in the place of torture and in the prison, in the assemblies of the poor—their unions, their leagues and their associations. It is also the prophetic word at the opportune moment. These are the actions which symbolise *participation*: the cathedral open to strikers, churches and chapels open to the peasants inland disputes, the walk that leads to a face to face encounter with the police or the soldiers.

In moments of confrontation even the mitre and the crosier regain their worth. It is not the power of excommunication which can check the fury of the torturers. When the forces of oppression are unchained, the bishop can become a rampart. His presence gives courage to the faltering and limits the audacity of the violent. There lives again St Ambrose and St John Chrysostom, St Athanasius and St Hilary. The phrase of Dom Helder Câmara, 'the voice of those with no voice' is a living reality.

Is this simply an exception, a special case? Is the presence of demonic forces so very exceptional in the world? Or indeed are the bishops so accustomed to them as a necessary part of the scenery—to the point where there is nothing to do, nothing to say? Is it not rather that the bishops have rediscovered their faith in their proper power in confronting a world which they find they have the courage to look full in the face?

The unfortunate remark of an Argentinian bishop who was asked why, when he knew, he remained silent: 'That would be a breach'—does this unhappy comment not betray what is to be found in the consciences of many prelates of traditional style? Episcopal power, is it not able to make a 'breach' when it needs to?

3. POWER IN THE INTERIOR OF THE CHURCH

So the powers of evil work their way into the interior of the Church. The modern idols of money, of domination, can also penetrate the Church. Then still the power of the Church is made available to it to flush out the enemy. The apostle Peter denounced Ananias and Saphira, Simon Magus; Paul denounced the apostles of compromise who betray the Gospel of the Cross. The prophets like Moses and Elijah already denounced penetration by demons in the form of idolatry. Then as today, it is the rich and the powerful who introduce them into the Church.

In the face of this penetration, the bishop still incarnates the resistance and the struggle against the powers of evil. Just as Christ denounces and unmasks the Pharisees, the false teachers and the false pastors, the bishop casts out the false pastors who present themselves in the form of the real seduction, those who offer the way of easy compromises.

Now, within the Christian community itself, composed as it is of righteous and sinners, strong and weak, beginners and adults in the faith, the behaviour of the Church is quite different. The gospels show us two faces of Jesus' power. There is a face for demons and another for sinners, the impoverished, the lame and those of no account. Towards the lost sheep of the house of Israel the power of Jesus shows itself as patience, encouragement, the capacity to raise the fallen and to give life to the dying.

We have also seen this style of power in Latin America. Bishops who with inexhaustible patience offer a welcome to multitudes of victims: poor, sick, without work, without education, without culture—multitudes who have never had any sort of religious formation, who have never known a family, who live from day to day. They know not to impose a heavy burden of ecclesiastical regulations on beings who are already weighed down on every side. They know that to poor Lazarus Jesus offers everything and demands nothing. They know that the power of God chooses his people from among the rejected of the earth. They open up the Church so that it does not become the refuge of the Pharisee and the symbol of a new Law.

This power shows itself in an infinite capacity to open arms, to open homes, and to open ways: to cause barriers and prejudice to crumble. It is the power to welcome the despised indigenous peoples, unremembered black slaves, peasants treated like cattle and exploited workers. It is the power which lowers barriers, destroys aggression, gives confidence to multitudes who have long learned to have no confidence in anyone at all. It is a power which the Church practises on itself: to require itself to be fully opened.

Yes, this does exist—now—in certain places in Latin America. It is not confined to the lives of saints of long ago.

Translated by James Aitken Gardiner

Sharon Holland

Attitudes of Heart and Mind

> There should be the closest possible coordination of all apostolic works and
> activities. This will depend mainly on a supernatural attitude of heart and
> mind grounded on charity. (CD 35.5)

FROM THE earliest centuries of Christianity, relationships between religious
and bishops have been in evolution. Much of this history is characterised by
the unfolding institution of exemption.[1] Today the teachings of Vatican II,
reflected in the 1983 Latin Code, offer new approaches to resolving old
tensions. Unity of purpose in the one mission of the Church calls for mutual
collaboration between two particular types of ecclesial office holder: diocesan
bishops and religious superiors.

Historically, by the fifth century, the random appearance on the scene of
monks and monasteries had become such a problem that the Council of
Chalcedon (451) established the requirement of episcopal permission for the
foundation of monasteries. Monks were made subject to bishops (c. 4).

It was recognised, however, that the communal nature of monasticism
required a certain independence in internal structures. The Rule of St Benedict
(d. 547) portrays the role of abbot as analogous to that of bishop. The abbot,
however, was not necessarily ordained since monasticism was not originally
viewed as clerical.

As monasticism became more involved in missionary activity, it became
more clerical. Not infrequently, monks were called forth from their personal
pursuit of holiness to undertake the exercise of episcopal authority.

As monasticism grew, strengthened, and centralised however, there were more frequent jurisdictional tensions with bishops. Pope Honorius I granted the first real exemption to the Irish monastery of Bobbio, Italy, in 628. By the early eleventh century, Cluny was subject to neither king nor bishop. In large part, however, monastic exemption was of *place*, with the abbot controlling the bishop's right of entrance to ordain or celebrate Mass.

As religious life became increasingly apostolic in orientation, it posed new questions of rapport with local ecclesiastical authority. The centralised structure and exemption of orders such as the Premonstratensians (twelfth century) and the Mendicants (thirteenth century) were often suspect among bishops; their preaching and encouragement of popular confraternities antagonised many among the secular clergy.

Councils, in turn, acted to limit exemption. At Constance (1414–1418), to remove anything derogatory to episcopal jurisdiction, all exemptions granted after the death of Gregory XI (1378) were revoked. Lateran V (1512–1517) pursuing charity and good will between bishops and religious orders, attempted to eliminate conflicts of jurisdiction. The Bull, *Dum Intra* (19 December 1516) protected the bishop's right of visitation at the parishes of regulars (n. 1) and his right to examine their candidates for orders (n. 10). The administration of sacraments by religious priests was regulated to protect the rights and prerogatives of pastors (nn. 16, 12).

In spite of this, in 1524, exemption was granted to the Theatines, one of the new orders of Clerks Regular. The exemption of the Jesuits in 1545 empowered them to preach and confer all sacraments, wherever they exercised ministry, without permission of the bishop.

The Council of Trent (1645–63) once again sought to impose limits. The Decree, *De Regularibus et Monialibus* (4 December 1563) addressing the care of souls and the administration of sacraments to seculars not of the religious household, held both secular and religious priests immediately subject to the jurisdiction, visitation, and correction of the diocesan bishop (C. XI). Cluny, however, was expected by name—as were others, depending on the status of the abbot or superior.

Over the centuries then, the institution of exemption which originally protected the internal, communal structures of cenobitic life, evolved into a method of keeping religious (expecially clerical) orders, available for papal mandates. This occasioned clashes with bishops; abuses periodically gave rise to attempts at reform. Nuns who were subject to the regular superiors shared somewhat in the exemption of place, but were not involved in apostolic ventures.

Lay apostolic congregations (men and women with simple vows) existed for centuries before they were technically recognised as religious. Only with Leo XIII's Apostolic Constitution, *Conditae a Christo* (1900) did these congregations gain juridic unity under superiors who possessed real authority throughout the institute. This added new categories of religious: in addition to exempt orders, there were pontificial and diocesan religious congregations serving in the local Church.

Following the teaching of Trent, and such documents as Leo XIII's Constitution *Romanos Pontifices* (8 May 1881), the 1917 Code reiterated the rather ambiguous status of religious exemption. These religious were removed from the jurisdiction of the local ordinary *praeterquam in casibus a iure expressis* (can. 615). The law itself granted exemption to Regulars (can. 615); it could be conceded to other religious (can. 618.1). Exempt clerical superiors had power of jurisdiction (can. 501 § 1). Exempt or not, pontifical institutes enjoyed greater protection from episcopal interventions (can. 618 § 2) than did diocesan.

After centuries of legislation, Vatican II built its expression of the relationship between bishops and religious on a renewed depth of theological reflection. Fundamental were its identification of the bishop as true pastor in the particular Church, and of religious life as a gift of the Spirit to the universal Church. A mixed commission drawn from *De Episcopis* and *De Religiosis* worked over articles of the draft *De Cura Animarum*, developing statements now reflected in *Lumen gentium* 45, *Christus Dominus*, 33–35 and Paul VI's Apostolic Letter, *Ecclesiae Sanctae*, 22–40. A key focus is pastoral care.

Lumen gentium states that the bishop's pastoral care of religious must be characterised by docility toward the Holy Spirit and respect for diverse founding charisms (45a). Exemption exists to better provide for the whole flock of Christ, but respect and obedience are still owed to bishops. This fosters unity and harmony in the apostolate.

Christus Dominus discusses religious among those who cooperate in the bishop's pastoral task. In the face of urgent pastoral need and the shortage of diocesan clergy, religious are viewed as part of the diocesan presbyterate and family. They are urged to increased collaboration (n. 34).

Exemption does not prevent religious from being subject to the jurisdiction of diocesan bishops, according to law, insofar as required for pastoral duties and the care of souls (n. 35.3). Rather, it pertains, first of all (*potissimum*), to the internal organisation of the institute. The listing of apostolic activities (n. 35.4) in which all religious, exempt or not, are subject to the local ordinary,is much more detailed than the paralleled statement from Trent. The norms in *Ecclesiae Sanctae* are even more so.

For the sake of good pastoral care, the bishop is responsible for fostering all possible co-ordination and collaboration within the local Church (n. 35.5, 6). This task requires an active awareness that religious life, as a gift to the Church, is expressed in multiple forms (PC 1; LG 43, 46). It enjoys its own unique way of life (PC 2; LG 43) while contributing to the needs of the Church (PC 8,10; CD 35).

In view of this belief that every institute is a gift to the universal Church, and subject to its supreme authority, some of those preparing the new Code believed exemption was no longer a useful category. Rather, autonomy sufficient for the protection of the institute's proper identity, spirit and mission was needed. While different from independence, this autonomy would guard against unwarranted external interventions and would be safeguarded by the local ordinary. Some saw this rightful autonomy and exemption as essentially the same.[2]

In the end, exemption was preserved, but no institutes are granted exemption by the law, and exempt status no longer differentiates between clerical institutes in the exercise of the power of governance (can. 596 § 2).

The same *coetus* which wrote of exemption (can. 591) and rightful autonomy (can. 586) also prepared canons on the role of religious in apostolic works. As ecclesial institutes, religious act by mandate of the Church and in ecclesial communion (can. 675 § 3); they are subject to their own superiors (can. 678 § 2) as well as to bishops in the 'care of souls, the public exercise of divine worship, and other works of apostolate' (can. 678 § 1). The collaboration called for by Vatican II and developed in *Mutuae relationes* (1978) is reflected in can. 678 § 3.

Commentaries on these canons[3] have begun to clarify an important distinction between rightful autonomy of life and exemption. Autonomy flows from the very nature of religious life as a gift of the Spirit, given to and received by the Church. Such autonomy is not created by the Code; it is an inherent necessity for preserving each institute's uniqueness, always within the Church. Hierarchical authority may neither ignore nor reject the Spirit's gifts; the recipients of new gifts may not ignore the Church's sacred ministers. Collaboration must take place because 'autonomy of life, especially of governance' (can. 586 § 1) is not exclusively in the realms of internal ordering. The founding charism informs the entire life of the institute, also giving shape to its share in the Church's mission.

Exemption, on the other hand, is a juridic construct and its use is dependent upon the free action of the Roman Pontiff. It serves to re-emphasise a special relationship to the Roman Pontiff, and reminds all of the universal mission of the Church which each bishop is to have at heart (CD 6). This, however, should not be seen as hindering full pastoral cooperation within the particular Church.

Collaboration in ministry and participation in diocesan structures (presbyteral council, pastoral council, synod) call both men and women religious into full communion with the needs, life, and structures of the local

Church. Simultaneously, the bishop must respect the gift which characterises each institute's particular life-style and approach to ministry. These attitudes of mutual respect and support require effort, but are essential. The rightful autonomy of institutes need not be lessened by the insertion of members into the local Church; likewise, the rightful authority of the diocesan bishop is not lessened by respect for religious autonomy. There will be tensions, but they must be resolved through collaboration for the sake of Christ's reign.

The experiences of history, and contemporary expressions of doctrine, suggest lines of reflection for the future.

1. Both hierarchical authority and religious charisms have been given to the Church for service, and the extension of Christ's mission. When both religious and bishops are focused on Christ and proclaiming the Gospel, the complementarity of diverse gifts can be recognised and collaboration is possible, despite tensions. However, when the focus of one or the other or both becomes the securing and consolidation of power, tensions become truly devisive. As a result, the real needs of the People of God are neglected.

2. Historically, tensions between religious and bishops were not primarily tensions between the ordained and the non-ordained. Often the greatest problems arose with regard to clerical exempt orders engaged in pastoral care. Legislation regarding exemption was only moderately successful in easing tensions. The 1983 Code's recognition of a rightful autonomy required by the very nature of every institute of consecrated life, provides a deeper foundation for truly mutual collaboration. The implications of c. 586 call for further study.

3. In the US, dialogues called for by the Papal Commission on Religious Life (1983–86) made an important beginning toward greater mutual understanding and respect between religious and bishops. The experience verified the Council statement that the close co-operation of religious and bishops would depend largely on an attitude of heart and mind grounded in charity.

Notes

1. E. Fogliasso, 'Exemption des Religieux', *Dictionnine de Droit Canonique* (Paris 1953–65), 5:646–66; 'Esenzione', *Dizionasio Instituti Perfectionio* III (Rome 1287–95).

2. *Communicationes* 5 (1973) 65; 7 (1975) 85–88.

3. J. Beyer, 'Religious and the Local Church', *Way Supplement 50* (1984) 80–98; R. Castillo-lara, 'De ecclesialitate vitae religiosae in Codice Iuris Canonici', *Periodica* 74 (1985) 419–37; V. Depaolis, 'Exemptio an Autonomia Institutorum Vitae Consecratae?' *Periodica* 71(1982) 147–78; G. Ghirlanda, 'La Vita Consacrata nella vita della Chiesa', *Informationes* 10 (1984) 79–96; R. Ombres, '*Iusta Autonomia Vitae*: Religious in the Local Church', *Clergy Review* 84 (1984) 310–19; E. Viganò, 'Carisma proprio e servizio Ecclesiale', *Informationea* 7 (1981) 214–37.

Piero Antonio Bonnet

Those with no Mandate in the Church

'All share a true equality with regard to the dignity and to the activity common to all the faithful' (LG 32c).[1]

ANY DISCUSSION of power in the Church, even when it can be restricted to a particular aspect, is inherently complex, if only because it is impossible to avoid some general assumptions. So, as it is my task here in a very short space to deal with the subject in so far as it relates to individuals whom the institution excludes from ministerial or hierarchical power, I feel that the best way to approach it will be to put forward various suggestions and to consolidate them with the help of selected and in my view very significant passages from Vatican II's Constitution on the Church.

The only possible point of departure for such a discussion is the *principle of equality* between all the faithful, which was so emphatically stated by Vatican II. In fact, the conciliar magisterium, tuning in admirably to the wavelength of our time, sought to highlight in a special way that unique communion which is the Church by means of the image of the 'People of God'. This image brings out the full force of the *common matrix* which binds all the faithful in Christ.

Vatican II (see LG 9a; 32b) and canon 205 of the 1983 Code of Canon Law define this common matrix as participation in the *same* word and the *same* sacraments in a *single* community. There exists in the Church, therefore, a vast fundamental equality, capable of embracing every aspect of the very rich life which goes on within the People of God. Even in the juridical economy of the

Church, the individual believer cannot but be the true and only *human protagonist*.[2]

Furthermore, this equality constitutes the common patrimony that the freedom which belongs to the believer by right, and which enables him creatively to forge his own way towards God, must successfully, and without harm, mould into forms most suited to it. As the one universal Church lives in the diversity of many local and particular churches (see LG 23a), so the one patrimony of faith-sacrament-community comes to life in the very diversity of the ways to God which individual believers, rooted in their particular churches, succeed in marking out, impressing on them the seal of their own, sometimes charismatic, individuality.

This, it seems to me, is how the fundamental provision ratified in canon 208 of the Code must be interpreted. Equality in the People of God means *unity in diversity*; that is, each believer constitutes an unassailably individual personification of the same redemptive patrimony, just as each man or woman is a particular and exclusive incarnation of the same humanity.[3]

II

'By divine institution Holy Church is structured and governed with a wonderful diversity' (LG 32a).

By bringing back into prominence the importance of equality in the Church, Vatican II intended to heal the division between clergy and laity which, the more it deepened in the context of canon law, the more incomprehensible it became. The division succeeded, in fact, on the one hand in concentrating the Church *almost* exclusively around the clergy, to whom alone it belonged to carry out the ecclesial mission, and on the other in so secularising the function of the laity that they were *almost* put outside the Church—so much so that they felt 'like outsiders, or else like an auxiliary workforce taken "into service" in times of overproduction, in order to do work which, properly speaking "is the concern of priests" '.[4]

The radical equality which still exists throughout the People of God compels us rather to regard the building up of the Church as the mission of all the faithful. Vatican II stressed this precisely in referring to the laity,[5] whom a theological and canonical culture then in vogue sought instead to exclude from this common responsibility: 'The laity are gathered together in the People of God and make up the Body of Christ under one Head. Whoever they are, they are called upon, as living members, to expend all their energy for the growth of the Church and its continuous sanctification' (LG 33a).

To accomplish this mission, the Church itself is 'by divine institution structured and governed with a wonderful diversity' (LG 32a). And it is precisely that variety of ministries, into which the single mission of the Church[6] divides in order to fulfil itself, that allows the faithful, without exception, to participate, each according to his particular gift, in the building up of the Church. Indeed, 'no part of the structure of a living body is merely passive but each has a share in the functions as well as in the life of the body. So too, in the Body of Christ, which is the Church, the whole body, "according to the functioning in due measure of each single part, derives its increase" (Eph. 4:16). Indeed, so intimately are the parts linked and interrelated in this body that the member who fails to make his proper contribution to the development of the Church must be said to be useful neither to the Church nor to himself' (AA 2a).

To get an immediate and flexible grasp of this key to the texts offered us by Vatican II, we can compare the many believers who make up the People of God to the wonderful variety of instruments in an immense orchestra as it plays a great symphony: each instrument, while it is essentially equal to every other as an object capable of producing sound when it vibrates, has in the particular timbre of the voice that can be drawn from it an unmistakable identity, which nevertheless merges with those of the others in a harmonious whole. In fact, from a functional point of view, each of these instruments, while remaining itself, lives during the performance in the harmony of the unitary accord to which it necessarily contributes, albeit in it own way. A false note from one leads to general disharmony, even when it is not detected by every ear. Each instrument, with its own sound, in its differentness, is equally necessary, even if not equally coresponsible as a cause of the unified result that is achieved.

III

'This diversity among its members arises ... by reason of their dutues' (LG 13c).

Although they all participate in the unique mission of the Church, the faithful do not all do so in the same measure. In fact, from the moment that each believer, 'by virtue of the very gifts bestowed upon him, is at the same time a witness and a living instrument of the mission of the Church herself, "according to the measure of Christ's bestowal" ' (LG 33b), it follows that coresponsibility for the carrying out of this necessary mission in the life of the Church, while it belongs to every member of the People of God, is not nevertheless measured according to a single standard.

More particularly, for the adequate and fitting exercise of the complex ministry of the Church, that is for the varied ensemble of homogeneous activities functionally directed to a particular end, personal ability—power subjectively expressed in a distinct way—is indispensable.[7] In fact, while the ministerial priesthood (hierarchical power) is needed for the development of certain ministries, for others the common priesthood is sufficient; and it is important, moreover, to remember that both forms of priesthood, 'though they differ from one another in essence and not only in degree, are nonetheless interrelated. Each of them in its own special way is a participation in the one priesthood of Christ' (LG 10b).

It is therefore only in terms of ability to carry out the mission of the Church that a qualitative differention (cf. LG 10b) comes into play between those who, because they are invested with hierarchical power, constitute the hierarchy properly so called and are in a position to practise an ordained ministry, and those who, because they do not possess this power, form the vast majority of the People of God—notably (although not exclusively, since account must be taken of non-ordained religious) the laity—and who are thus suited to carrying out a mission that is no less essential ecclesially speaking (cf. Rom. 12:4–5), even though it is 'non-ordained'. More particularly, therefore, in the People of God, as Vatican II teaches, 'each individual part contributes through its special gifts to the good of the other parts and of the whole Church. Thus through the common sharing of gifts and through the common effort to obtain fulness in unity, the whole and each of the parts receive increase. Not only, then, is the People of God made up of different peoples but even in its inner structure it is composed of various ranks. This diversity among its members arises either by reason of their duties ["secundum officia"], as is the case with those who exercise the sacred ministry for the good of their brethren, or by reason of their situation and way of life' (LG 13c).

In this way, with an ecclesiological statement the canonical importance of which is obvious, the council, without altering in the least way its essential radical truth, transcends the preconciliar dualism which set the clergy in opposition to the rest of the People of God, the laity in particular.[8] More precisely, the conciliar magisterium envisages a harmonious insertion of the bipolarity constituted by the two priesthoods into the organic unity formed from the plurality of ministries which characterises the People of God, asserting moreover a capability which, even when it presupposes hierarchical power is 'a true service, and in sacred literature is significantly called "diakonia" or ministry' (LG 24a).

IV

'There is in Christ and in the Church no inequality on the basis of race or nationality, social condition or sex' (LG 32b).

Those, therefore, among the People of God who do not possess ministerial priesthood are nevertheless capable of whatever ministry is not bound to that priesthood, by virtue of a power of their own that is rooted in the sacraments and the Church,[9] even though it is qualitatively and therefore essentially different from hierarchical power. However, this purely functional differentiation, correctly understood, does nothing to destroy the fundamental equality which unites the faithful in the People of God. Indeed, that essential diversification notwithstanding, Augustine was able to say: 'For you I am a bishop, with you I am a Christian'.[10] And, as the same Augustine added: 'What we are for ourselves is one thing, what we are for you is another. As far as we personally are concerned, we are Christians, even though for you we are clerics and bishops.'[11]

The truth is that the fundamental condition shared by all the People of God, which is firmly rooted, as we have seen, in the principle of equality, must tend to exclude any categorisation, beyond what is proper to the individual believer, on the basis of *status*—any differentiation, that is, of a personal nature that becomes binding under canon law. For the rest, while not wishing to exaggerate the importance of a juridical qualification, it is precisely around the canonical notion of 'status' that it was possible to establish in the People of God the assertion, to which attention has already been drawn, of a clear division—not to say a separation—between clergy and laity. In the context of the unique 'status' of believer, it is more necessary today than ever to examine thoroughly (which is clearly not possible here) the diversity 'secundum officia', redetermining according to the needs of the time the identity of the complex and multi-faceted ecclesial ministry. This is especially true of the ordained ministry, around which the Church is brought together in a particular way. To that end, it seems to me that what is needed above all is an adequate objective characterisation of it, based on the Word of God historically incarnate in the Church of our own time. In fact, characterisation by function will only be adequate in so far as it allows for an appropriate characterisation, *subjectively*-speaking, of those who, because of their particular gifts, are called to the ordained ministry by God. To my way of thinking, serious reflection on the matter cannot but tend towards a sharp reduction of this form of ministry, which in any case, since Vatican II and the new Code of Canon Law, is already a reality—even though a certain amount of progress still needs to be made. This quantative—not qualitative—reorganisation of the ordained ministry will be very beneficial, allowing clerics to devote themselves wholeheartedly, *principally* if not exclusively, *to the ministries which, exclusively and without exception*, are uniquely theirs. Such a restriction of function will contribute in a significant though naturally not dramatic way to the overcoming of a crisis of numbers where vocations to the ministerial priesthood are concerned—a crisis which, despite certain negative elements, has nevertheless had the advantage of reversing a tendency towards excessive clericalisation in the Church.

This reorganisation of the ordained ministry requires a corresponding organisation of the non-ordained ministry. Any reorganisation of the condition of ministry encourages us to search for new balances and consequently for new and original forms of coordination and collaborations between the two forms of ministry. On the other hand, it goes without saying that relations between these different forms of ministry will not always be easy, since it will not always be possible to avoid the friction that arises from uncertainty about the spheres of activity proper to each—uncertainty caused not least by the vagueness of the existing Code in this respect. Mistakes will inevitably be made, but it is essential, as we have seen, that those who are called more particularly to a non-hierarchical ministry, notably the laity, should be given 'time and space, under the guidance and rule of authority, to feel their way towards their specific function in the Church, since they too are placed under the grace of the Holy Spirit'.[12]

Within this framework, it must also be possible to show how, in the Church, each believer occupies a position of his own, clearly defined according to the specific task—i.e., to the ministry—which it is his to perform. What is more, it must be shown that although the diversity of ministries only exists because people receive different gifts from God, this does not make it any the less necessary, since all ministries have a precise raison d'etre in the economy of the Church.

All this requires, however, that ministry—especially non-ordained ministry—should be treated seriously—that is rigorously and courageously—in ecclesial law. It is therefore necessary that in theory and above all in practice the numerous ecclesially unjustifiable barriers that confront the laity, women in particular, should be removed, allowing them all—men and women—access to the non-ordained ministry, assuming of course that they possess the requisite charisms. There is no theological foundation, at least in this context, for discrimination based on sex, which cannot be justified except on grounds of timeliness, and, as in the case mentioned in canon 230, § 1, it is difficult, if not impossible, at the present time to find a truly persuasive argument in favour of that. In short, lay people, particularly the women among them, must be able to be and to feel that they *as such* are the Church, that is 'subjects fully endowed with faith and responsible for it, and responsible too for expressing it and bearing witness to it'.[13] In this way it will be possible for the Church to evaluate fully an aspect of ministry which is by no means negligible but which today tends to be treated as alternative.[14]

In this canonical line of development, it is necessary to remove every material obstacle that might prevent people from entering or exercising the ministry of the Church—notably conditions that lead to their marginalisation, in society or in the Church. Much could be done to overcome such attitudes—and this is necessary in relation to ministry as well as in itself—were subjective juridical positions (rights-duties) to be given canonical studies. Such positions, by giving to that end an active voice to the interested parties themselves, could constitute the consolidation moment for special juridical disciplines in this connection,[15] given that merely to emphasise duty in the general way that it applies to all believers, in terms of activity concentrated on combating such conditions of marginalisation, as in the case mentioned in canon 222 § 2, can no longer claim to be adequate or sufficient.

Indeed, a serious effort to realise ministry in the spirit of Vatican II will ensure that those who live in the common priesthood only no longer experience their position in a predominantly *negative* way, in a perspective that is reflected in the title of this article. The way towards this—which is why I have preferred a largely *positive* formulation—is already opened up in the 1983 Code, even though much still needs to be done to make more common among the People of God a condition that *prophetically* speaking is already proper to certain ecclesial groups who live 'an ordinary life in accordance with the Gospel, without any distinction between married or single, men or women. These believers form communities in which there is room for married people as well as for those who have deliberately chosen the celibate life. They prefer minimal structures, in which, apart from a certain measure of privacy for individuals and families, attention is focused entirely on the life of the community ... The bond between all the members, brothers and sisters, is dominant, even though differences of function and ecclesial ministry are recognised. Their great concern is to get rid of the old "status-based" model ... . Here, Gospel and humanity are not two separate realities: all work with a Christian humanity that is growing, if still incomplete.'[16]

Translated by Sarah Fawcett

Notes

1. The passages from the documents of Vatican II will be identified by the initial letters of the first Latin words of the document from which they are taken. The English

translation used here is: Walter M. Abbott SJ (Ed.) *The Documents of Vatican II* (London 1966).

2. For a more detailed examination of this point see my 'Il "christifidelis" recuperato protagonista umano nella Chiesa', in AA.VV, *Vaticano II. Bilanicio e prospettive 25 anni dopo*, ed. R. Latourelle (Assisi 1987).

3. E. Schillebeeckx *The Mission of the Church* (London 19??) p. 291 (*De Zending van de Kerk. Theologischen Peilingen*, IV, Bilthoven 1970).

4. For fuller treatment, see what I have said elsewhere: 'Habet pro conditione dignitatem libertatemque filiorum Dei', in *Il diritto ecclesiastico* (1981) No. 92/1, pp. 556–620; 'De christifidelium communi statu', *Periodica* (1982) No. 71, pp. 463–529; 'De omnium christifidelium obligationibus et iuribus', in P. A. Bonnet/G. Ghirlanda *De Christifidelibus* (Rome 1983) pp. 21–52; entry 'Fedeli' in *Enciclopedia Giuridica* (Rome, to be published by the Istituto dell'Enciclopedia Italiana).

5. See P. A. Bonnet 'De laicorum notione adumbratio', in *Periodica* (1985) No. 74, pp. 259–264, and 'La ministerialità laicale', in AA.VV. *Teologia e diritto canonico* (Città del Vaticano 1987) pp. 87–130.

6. See what I have written elsewhere ('Est in Ecclesia diversitas ministerii sed unitas missionis', in AA.VV. *Les droits fondamentaux du Chrétien* (Fribourg 1981) pp. 291–308), and for a more general and wide-ranging discussion in which this point is taken up see the entry 'Pluralismo (in genere): a) diritto canonico', in *Enciclopedia del diritto* vol. 33 (Milan 1983) pp. 956–983.

7. For a discussion of the complex problem of the origin of hierarchical power, see P. A. Bonnet 'Diritto e potere nel momento originario della "potestas hierarchica" nella Chiesa', in *Ius canonicum* (1975) No. 15/29, pp. 75–157, and 'Una questione ancora aperta: l'origine del potere gerarchico nella Chiesa', in *Ephemerdies iuris canonici* (1982) No. 38, pp. 62–121.

8. See J. Beyer 'Laïcat ou Peuple de Dieu', in AA.VV. *La Chiesa dopo il Concilio* vol. II/1 (Milan 1972) pp. 233–247.

9. See P. A. Bonnet 'La ministerialità laicale', (see note 5 above), pp. 126–130.

10. *Sermo* 340, n. 1.

11. *Sermo* 301, n. 8.

12. E. Schillebeeckx *The Mission of the Church* (see note 3 above), p. 179.

13. E. Schillebeeckx (London 1986) p. 000 (*Pleidooi voor Mensen in de Kerk*, Baarn 1985).

14. *Ibid.* pp. 289–292.

15. For a paradigmatically significant case, see my contribution, 'Una dimenticanza del codice di diritto canonico del 1983: il diritto-dovere fondamentale del fedele migrante', in AA.VV. *Raccolta di scritti in memoria di Raffaele Moschella* (Perugia 1985) pp. 87–125.

16. E. Schillebeeckx (see note 13 above) p. 289.

Stephen Sykes

Power in the Church of England

THIS ESSAY concerns the distribution and exercise of power in one non-Catholic church, namely the Church of England. We are speaking here not of Anglicanism as a whole, but of a part of that communion of churches, each of which has made its own particular settlement of the organisational problems common to all Christian churches. The subject has to be studied historically, because, as we shall see, certain characteristically Anglican tensions are inexplicable apart from the history in which they are embedded. There is a further reason for the historical approach. The Church of England is established by law. But because England has no written constitution, there is no one document to which we can refer in order to understand the relationship between Church and State. The 'establishment' has, as a matter of fact been progressively modified in every century since the sixteenth, up to very recent times.[1]

I

The theology of power in the Church of England (and by speaking of 'power' we simply follow the usage of the English Reformation) has concerned relationships between four major partners. The first, the *sovereign*, both retained and enlarged powers already traditional since the days of Hincmar (c. 806–882), the innovatory Archbishop of Reims. The sovereign was understood to have received a divine charism for the work of government, and promised to 'study to preserve thy people committed to his charge' (Prayer Book Collect from 1549). At the same time, in England the Acts of Supremacy establishing the sovereign's position were Acts of *Parliament*, who

123

thus constituted the second of the major partners. Under Elizabeth I Parliament was indeed given a role in the determination of what constitutes heresy. The third partner was, of course, the *episcopate*, of which more will be said below. Finally, a role was preserved for bishops and priests in *synodical association* (known traditionally as Convocation), to which was added in 1885 a lay assembly, superseded in 1920 by the Church Assembly and in 1970 by General Synod, the last two incorporating bishops, ordinary clergy and lay people.

In various configurations these four partners have constituted for the Church of England what should be termed the 'higher participants' in the organisation.[2] For most of the history of the Church of England lay involvement in the power élites has been restricted to a governing class, that is members of the Houses of Lords and of Commons and, throughout the country, prominent landowners who exercised considerable powers of patronage and control over local clergy. The mass of lay people have traditionally been exhorted to be submissive and to live quiet and godly lives, in accordance with New Testament instruction. For their part, bishops and clergy at their ordinations have been presented with a strongly pastoral (rather than sacramental or disciplinary) model of their office, following the advice of Martin Bucer (1491–1551) and reflecting the stance of the Pastoral Epistles.

The Church of England's retention of the historic episcopate and threefold office was a form of practical conservatism which only slowly hardened into explicit theological expression. The catalyst here was the development by Theodore Beza (1519–1605) of the argument that the presbyteral church order was alone of divine origin and sanction. In opposition Anglican writers of the late sixteenth century began to support the view that the threefold office could be found in the New Testament and be traced back to the apostles. The defence of episcopacy also rested heavily on critical work on the Epistles of Ignatius which were closely studied and edited by Anglican scholars in the 1640s. An influential theologian, Henry Hammond, defended in 1647 the Ignatian view that the bishop, seated on his throne, was the very image of Christ, exercising an authority committed by Christ to his apostles, and handed on by them to their successors, the Catholic episcopate.[3] A rubric in the 1662 Book of Common Prayer insisted that episcopal consecration was the *sine qua non* to holding ministerial office in the Church of England.

The sociological outcome of these developments is complex. The episcopate had been retained, but its power had been shared with lay 'higher participants'. A polemical situation had developed (anti-presbyterianism) which led to the alignment of the Anglican episcopate with that of other episcopal churches. But the power structures themselves did not change. On the contrary, the Anglican episcopate was increasingly drawn into the party politics of the late seventeenth and early eighteenth century English state. The defence of an Ignatian theology of the episcopate had little practical outcome, except in the rejection of the ministries of the non-episcopal churches of the Continent. Neither the pastoral interpretation of Martin Bucer, nor the monarchical interpretation of the devotees of Ignatius, were therefore given consistent public expression in the practice of episcopacy.

II

A tension thus was established within the Church of England between the practical recognition of lay jurisdictional power, and the potential for a strong development of the power of orders. The nineteenth-century Oxford Movement, led by, among others, John Henry Newman (1801–1890), took full advantage of this possibility. It interpreted the religious situation in England of the 1830s as entailing a stark choice between the authority of Parliament and the spiritual authority of the church. The prestige of the priesthood, Newman argued, had hitherto relied too much on birth, education and wealth; it was now time to return to the priesthood's 'apostolical descent', and the ordained were instructed to 'magnify your office'.[4] The separation from reliance upon Parliament which this clarion call implied facilitated the exceptionally rapid growth of the Anglican Communion overseas.[5]

In nineteenth-century England, the power of the episcopate, though theoretically strengthened in the post-Oxford movement Church, continued to be challenged from within the élite group of 'higher participants'. This happened for two reasons. First, there remained a strong tradition of involvement in church affairs by a lay élite, working through Parliament, lay patronage or Church organisations of various tendencies. Among these, of course, was a prominent group of lay people with Evangelical sympathies, unpersuaded by Tractarian theology and by the 'priest-craft' to which it was thought to give rise. But, secondly, a curious feature of Tractarianism must also be observed, which has persisted in the Church of England to the present, namely, a deeply engrained ambivalence towards the authority of the episcopate itself. Thus although Newman, as an Anglican, spoke of 'our Holy Fathers, the Bishops' as 'the Representatives of the Apostles and the Angels of the Churches', in fact if a Bishop resisted the theology and practices of the Tractarians he was resolutely opposed.[6]

Sociologically this situation can only be defined as the development of a sense that the priesthood itself belonged to the 'higher participants' of the organisation. This is a conviction evidently shared by all theological tendencies within the Anglican priesthood, and might well be called 'priestly congregationalism'. A priest with a secure power-base in his own congregation (or, in recent times, in the book trade, radio or television) can feel entitled publicly to discuss or even challenge statements from episcopal sources. Priests who achieve notoriety by these means often seek election to the synods of the church.

III

Governing the Church of England under such conditions has proved to be exceptionally difficult, especially since the bitter controversies of the nineteenth century. The 1860s and 70s were decades during which priests and congregations of Anglo-catholic persuasion struggled to establish their legal right to adopt the language, vestments and practices associated with the eucharistic sacrifice. The opposition was prepared to fight them all the way to the law courts and tribunals of the State, whose right to decide such matters was, of course, denied by the successors to the Tractarians.

It was at this time that a semi-official ideology of Anglicanism rose to prominence, at least partly in order to assist the 'higher participants' in curbing partisan excesses. According to this theory the history of the Church of England exemplifies three tendencies, the protestant-evangelical, appealing primarily to scripture, the catholic-tractarian appealing to tradition, and the latitudinarian-liberal stressing the role of reason. Each tendency was seen as coming to particular prominence in the nineteenth century, but each had earlier antecedents. All the tendencies are necessary to each other, so the ideology ran, and together they constitute the 'comprehensiveness' of the Church of England. They must, therefore, be held in some kind of tension or equilibrium, each belonging together as facets of a larger truth.

The sponsorship of a semi-official ideology of 'comprehensiveness' structuring the complex history of the Church of England has obvious managerial attractions. But it tends to disguise the interests of those who stand most to gain from its currency, namely, the episcopate and the bureaucracy. It is proper, therefore, to speak also of the 'bureaucratic party' of the Church of England. Identification of this party helps to explain the otherwise puzzling fact that the episcopate is overwhelmingly not composed of clearly identifiable 'party men', in the traditional sense. They are enlisted largely from those who have shown an ability to manage divergent tendencies, in parishes, or seminaries or senior administrative appointments. Similarly identifiable would be a large number of highly qualified lay people, including women, who participate in the highest ranks of the governing élite of the Church of England, and whose presence replaces to a large degree the traditional influence of lay members of Parliament.

IV

In 1970 the Church of England replaced its earlier structures of government with a General Synod, consisting of three 'Houses', of bishops, clergy (including women deacons) and laity. This development was, in effect, the repatriation into England of the synodical government of other parts of the Anglican communion, though without the final achievement of autonomy.

Outside and inside the General Synod Anglicans of various convictions continue to debate publicly all the major moral and doctrinal questions of the day, such as nuclear armaments, abortion and the ethics of genetic experimentation, the remarriage of the divorced, homosexuality, the resurrection, the divinity of Christ, the ordination of women to the priesthood, and the controversial issues raised by bilateral ecumenical dialogues. Although certain matters relating to doctrine, liturgy and the sacraments are only capable of being approved in terms proposed by the House of Bishops, the General Synod is perceived to be an open forum in which dissent from episcopal judgment is permissible; public disagreeemnt between bishops is not thought to be a scandal.

The adoption of parliamentary-type procedures in General Synod has tended to exacerbate the divisions between the traditional parties, though on some questions conservatives of differing traditions have allied against liberal or progressive opinion, for example, on the issue of the ordination of women to the priesthood. It is notable that on this question in particular the positive opinion of the House of Bishops has been twice successfully resisted by the clergy. This fact confirms my analysis that priests elected to synods see themselves as having the power appropriate to 'higher participants'.

V

The theological interpretation and criticism of this situation is, needless to say, a task of very considerable complexity. The Church of England cannot call on one traditional exposition of the significance of the episcopal office. The assertions of the Prayer Book that the three offices are manifestly to be found in the New Testament are challengeable, and the Episcopal Church of the United States has, in fact, modified this claim in its new Book of Common Prayer. The lack of a dogmatic tradition in this matter may be an advantage at a time when biblical research is forcing theology to re-evaluate both structures and their legitimations.

Four brief comments on this situation must be made. The public spectacle of a church in open integral disagreement is widely thought to be a handicap to its mission. But it is possible that what is fatal to the Church is not so much the mere fact of dispute as rancorous dispute, bad feeling, and party-spirit. It is also conceivable that fear of being made a public spectacle will tempt the 'bureaucratic party' to engage in extensive covert manipulation of the course and outcome of debate.

Secondly, the mention of manipulation draws attention to the importance of the control of the means of communication. Churches are systems of communication, in which bureaucrats necessarily become expert. If there is to be debate in the Church, it is essential that the means of communication are not dominated by those whose decisions will prevail.

Thirdly, parliamentary or democratic analogies may mislead the Church into the unthinking acceptance of lobbying by sectional interests as a normal mode of procedure. There is a fundamental contradiction between such ideas and the representativeness of the ordained ministry.

Finally, the Church of England has inherited from the Reformation a tradition of Christian nurture by active participation in the public worship of the Church. It has not yet with any conspicuous success developed this valuable resource into a theology of the whole people of God. If it were to join such a project with a sociologically realistic analysis of its current distribution and exercise of power, the ecumenical contribution might well be of some significance.

Notes

1. There have been no less than four reports on the relationship of Church and State in England in the twentieth century alone: in 1917, 1935, 1952, and 1970.

2. The term is adopted from Amitai Etzioni's analysis of organisation in *A Comparative Analysis of Complex Organizations* (Free Press of Glencoe 1961) esp. pp. 3–21.

3. See J. W. Packer *The Transformation of Anglicanism 1643–1660* (Manchester 1969).

4. J. H. Newman Tract I in *Tracts for the Times* Vol I (London 1835) p. 4.

5. See P. H. E. Thomas 'A Family Affair: The Pattern of Constitutional Authority in the Anglican Communion' in S. W. Sykes (ed.) *Authority in the Anglican Communion* (Toronto 1987) pp. 119–143.

6. See S. W. Sykes and S. W. Gilley 'No Bishop, No Church: The Tractarian impact on Anglicanism' in G. Rowell (ed.) *Tradition Renewed* (London 1986) p. 131.

Contributors

JOSEF BLANK was born 8 September 1926 in Ludwigshafen am Rhein and studied at Tübingen, Munich and Würzburg. Since 1969 he has been professor of New Testament exegesis and Biblical Theology at the Saarland University, Saarbrücken. Among his publications are *Krisis* (1964), *Paulus und Jesus* (1968), *Das Evangelium als Garantie der Freiheit* (1970), *Der Mensch am Ende der Moral* (1971), *Christliche Orientierungen* (1981).

P. A. BONNET, who has degrees in jurisprudence and canon law and a diploma in paleography, is associated professor of canon law and temporary professor of ecclesiastical law at the University of Modena and visiting professor in the faculty of canon law at the Pontifical Gregorian University. He has written entries for various encyclopaedias, and contributed numerous articles to specialist journals, notably *Ephemerides iuris canonici, Periodica* and *Il diritto ecclesiastico* (of the editorial board of which he is a member). His monographs include *L'Essenza del matrimonio canonico* (1976); *Scuola a sgravio e pluralismo scolastico* (1979); *Introduzione al consenso matrimoniale canonico* (1985).

JOSEPH COMBLIN was born in Brussels in 1923 and ordained in 1947. He has worked in Latin America since 1958, in particular Brazil and Chile. He has also taught at the University of Louvain. Recent publications include: *O tempo da ação* (1982); *A força da palavra* (1987); *Curso breve de teologia*, 4 vol., ed. Paul (1983–86); *Antropologia cristã* (1985); *O Espírito Santo e a libertação* (1987); *Epístola aos Filipenses* (1985); *Epístola aos Colossenses* (1986); *Epístola aos Efésios* (1987) in the *Comentário bíblico* de Vozes, Petrópolis.

ERIC FUCHS was born in Geneva in 1932. He has been a pastor of the Reformed Church since 1958. He is a doctor of theology and has been director of the Protestant Study Centre in Geneva since 1979. He was professor of ethics in the theological faculty of the University of Lausanne from 1981 to 1987. Since then he has been professor of ethics in the theological faculty of the University of Geneva. Among his main works are: *Le Désir et la tendresse* (1979): Eng. tr., 1983; *Initiation à la pratique de la théologie* (1983), Vol. IV, *Ethics*: 'Une ethique chretienne de la sexualité'; Au nom de l'Autre. Essai sur le fondement des droits de l'homme (1985) (with P.-A. Stucki); *La Morale selon Calvin* (1986).

KARL GABRIEL was born in 1943 and studied theology at Tübingen and sociology at Frankfurt and Bielefeld. Since 1980 he has been professor of sociology at the Catholic College for North Germany at Osnabrück and Vechta. Among his publications are: *Analysen der Organisations-gesellschaft* (1979); edited together with F. X. Kaufmann *Zur Soziologie des Katholizismus* (1980); 'Religionssoziologie als Soziologie des Christentums' in F. Daiber and T. Luckmann (ed.) *Religion in den Hauptströmungen der deutschen Soziologie* (1982); together with F. X. Kaufmann 'Catholicism in the German-speaking Countries' in T. Gannon (ed.) *World Catholicism in Transition* (1988).

PATRICK GRANFIELD was born in 1930. He has a doctorate in philosophy from the Pontifical Institute of St Anselm in Rome and in theology from the Catholic University of America. He teaches systematic theology, specialising in ecclesiology, at the Catholic University of America. His recent publications include *Ecclesial Cybernetics: A Study of Democracy in the Church* (1973), *The Papacy in Transition* (1980) with revised edition in German *Das Papsttum: Kontinuität und Wandel* (1984), and *The Limits of the Papacy: Authority and Autonomy in the Church* (1987).

SHARON HOLLAND, IHM is Assistant Professor of Canon Law at the Catholic University of America. She served as a consultant to the Papal Commission on Religious Life in the US.

JOHN E. LYNCH, born 1924 in New York, was ordained a priest in the Paulist Fathers community in 1951. Licentiate in Medieval Studies at the Pontifical Institute of Mediaeval Studies in Toronto 1959. Doctor of Philosophy, University of Toronto 1965. Professor of the History of Canon Law and Medieval History at The Catholic University of America from 1966. He has served as Chairman of the Canon Law Department (1974–83) and of the History Department (1983–86); Vice-President of the Canon Law Society of America and of the Executive Council of the American Catholic Historical Association. The Franciscan Institute published his study, *The Theory of Knowledge of Vital du Four*. 'He has published articles in *The Jurist, The Journal of Ecumenical Studies, Chicago Studies, The Encyclopedia of Religion,* and *The New Catholic Encyclopedia* of which he was area editor for canon and civil law for Vol. 17 supplement.

AUGUSTINE MENDONCA was born in Mangalore, India, in 1941. He completed his philosophical and theological studies at St Joseph's Seminary, Mangalore. After his oridnation in 1966, he worked as an Associate Pastor in the Diocese of Mangalore and then in the Diocese of Montego Bay, Jamaica, WI. He is a judge of the Toronto Regional Matrimonial Tribunal and a psychological consultant to several matrimonial courts across Canada. At present he is an Assistant Professor of Canon Law at Saint Paul University, Canada. His publications include: 'Antisocial Personality and Nullity of Marriage', *Studia Canonica* 15 (1981) 45–72; 'Schizophrenia and Nullity of Marriage', *Studia Canonica* 17 (1983) 197–237; 'A New Jurisprudential Aspect of Antisocial Personality Disorder in Relation to Marriage', *Catholic Lawyer* Vol. 29, No. 1 (1984) 22–32; 'The Effects of Personality Disorders on Matrimonial Consent' *Studia Canonica* 21 (1987); 'The Effects of Multiple Sclerosis on Matrimonial Consent', in *Studia Canonica* 21 (1987).

HERVI RIKHOF was born in 1948 in Oldenzaal. He studied theology in Utrecht and Oxford, graduated in 1981 and was ordained in 1985. He now teaches dogmatic theology in the theological faculty of the Catholic University of Nijmegen. His publications include the following in the sphere of ecclesiology and Vatican II: *The Concept of the Church* (1981); 'De ecclesiologieën van LG, LEF en Schema CIC' Concilium (1981) no. 17, 66–75; 'De kerk als "communio": een zinnige uitspraak?' Tijdschrift voor Theologie (1983), No. 23, 1, 39–59; '*Corpus Christi Mysticum.* An Inquiry into Thomas Aquinas' Use of the Term' Bijdragen (1976) No. 37, 2, 149–171; 'The Necessity of Church. An Exploration' *Archivio di Filosofia* (1986) No. 54, 481–500 (*Colloquium Intersoggestività, Socialità, Religione*).

WIGAND SIEBEL was born in 1929 in Freudenberg, Westphalia. Since 1965 he has held a chair of sociology at the Uniersity of Saarbrücken. Publications include *Die Logik des Experiments in den Sozialwissenschaften* (1965); *Freiheit und Herrschaftsstruktur in der Kirche* (1971); *Einführung in die systematische Soziologie* (1974); *Grundlagen der Logik* (1975); (together with Wolfgang Rau and Peter Kleinmann) *Herrschaft und Liebe—Zur Soziologie der Familie* (1984); *Der Heilige Geist als Relation—Eine soziale Trinitätslehre* (1986).

STEPHEN SYKES was born in 1939 and studied theology at Cambridge and Harvard. He was ordained in the Church of England in 1964, and was Fellow and Dean of St John's College, Cambridge and University Lecturer in Divinity from 1964 to 1974. For eleven years from 1975 to 1985 he taught systematic theology in University of Durham as Van Mildert Canon Professor. In 1985 he was elected Regius Professor of Divinity in the University of Cambridge. He is the author of numerous books and articles, including *The Integrity of Anglicanism* (1979) and *The Identity of Christianity*

(1985), and has edited (with J. Booty) *The Study of Anglicanism* to be published in 1988.

RIK TORFS was born at Turnhout, Belgium, in 1956. He studied at Louvain and Strasbourg universities. He has degrees in jurisprudence and advocacy, and a doctorate in canon law. He is attached to Louvain University and is also a guest lecturer at Utrecht Catholic University. He is co-founder of the working group of Dutch-language canonists (WNC). He is the author of some forty publications on canon law, Church and State, and secular family property law, including the following books: *De vrouw en het kerkelyk ambt. Analyse in functie van de mensenrechteen en Kerk en Staat* [on women, ecclesiatical office and human rights] (Leuven 1985); *International Testament*, co-author, (1985); *Het nieuwe kerkelijk recht* [on the new Code of canon law] Ed. (1985); *Het canonieke huwelijksbegrip* [on the concept of marriage in canon law] (1987).

PATRICK VALDRINI was born in 1947 at Saint-Mihiel (Meuse). He is at present dean of the faculty of canon law in Paris and president of the International Society of canon law and comaprative religious law. Since 1986 he has been editor of the review *L'Année Canonique*. His publications include, besides articles and notes concerning the problems of administrative canon law *Conflits et recours dans l'Eglise* (1978) and *Injustices et protection des droits dans l'Eglise* (1983).

CONCILIUM

1. (Vol. 1 No. 1) **Dogma.** Ed. Edward Schillebeeckx. 86pp.
2. (Vol. 2 No. 1) **Liturgy.** Ed. Johannes Wagner. 100pp.
3. (Vol. 3 No. 1) **Pastoral.** Ed. Karl Rahner. 104pp.
4. (Vol. 4 No. 1) **Ecumenism.** Hans Küng. 108pp.
5. (Vol. 5 No. 1) **Moral Theology.** Ed. Franz Bockle. 98pp.
6. (Vol. 6 No. 1) **Church and World.** Ed. Johannes Baptist Metz. 92pp.
7. (Vol. 7 No. 1) **Church History.** Roger Aubert. 92pp.
8. (Vol. 8 No. 1) **Canon Law.** Ed. Teodoro Jimenez Urresti and Neophytos Edelby. 96pp.
9. (Vol. 9 No. 1) **Spirituality.** Ed. Christian Duquoc. 88pp.
10. (Vol. 10 No. 1) **Scripture.** Ed. Pierre Benoit and Roland Murphy. 92pp.
11. (Vol. 1 No. 2) **Dogma.** Ed. Edward Shillebeeckx. 88pp.
12. (Vol. 2 No. 2) **Liturgy.** Ed. Johannes Wagner. 88pp.
13. (Vol. 3 No. 2) **Pastoral.** Ed. Karl Rahner. 84pp.
14. (Vol. 4 No. 2) **Ecumenism.** Ed. Hans Küng. 96pp.
15. (Vol. 5 No. 2) **Moral Theology.** Ed. Franz Bockle. 88pp.
16. (Vol. 6 No. 2) **Church and World.** Ed. Johannes Baptist Metz. 84pp.
17. (Vol. 7 No. 2) **Church History.** Ed. Roger Aubert. 96pp.
18. (Vol. 8 No. 2) **Religious Freedom.** Ed. Neophytos Edelby and Teodoro Jimenez Urresti. 96pp.
19. (Vol. 9 No. 2) **Religionless Christianity?** Ed. Christian Duquoc. 96pp.
20. (Vol. 10 No. 2) **The Bible and Tradition.** Ed. Pierre Benoit and Roland E. Murphy. 96pp.
21. (Vol. 1 No. 3) **Revelation and Dogma.** Ed. Edward Schillebeeckx. 88pp.
22. (Vol. 2 No. 3) **Adult Baptism and Initiation.** Ed. Johannes Wagner. 96pp.
23. (Vol. 3 No. 3) **Atheism and Indifference.** Ed. Karl Rahner. 92pp.
24. (Vol. 4 No. 3) **The Debate on the Sacraments.** Ed. Hans Küng. 92pp.
25. (Vol. 5 No. 3) **Morality, Progress and History.** Ed. Franz Bockle. 84pp.
26. (Vol. 6 No. 3) **Evolution.** Ed. Johannes Baptist Metz. 88pp.
27. (Vol. 7 No. 3) **Church History.** Ed. Roger Aubert. 92pp.
28. (Vol. 8 No. 3) **Canon Law—Theology and Renewal.** Ed. Neophytos Edelby and Teodoro Jimenez Urresti. 92pp.
29. (Vol. 9 No. 3) **Spirituality and Politics.** Ed. Christian Duquoc. 84pp.
30. (Vol. 10 No. 3) **The Value of the Old Testament.** Ed. Pierre Benoit and Roland Murphy. 92pp.
31. (Vol. 1 No. 4) **Man, World and Sacrament.** Ed. Edward Schillebeeckx. 84pp.
32. (Vol. 2 No. 4) **Death and Burial: Theology and Liturgy.** Ed. Johannes Wagner. 88pp.
33. (Vol. 3 No. 4) **Preaching the Word of God.** Ed. Karl Rahner. 96pp.
34. (Vol. 4 No. 4) **Apostolic by Succession?** Ed. Hans Küng. 96pp.
35. (Vol. 5 No. 4) **The Church and Social Morality.** Ed. Franz Bockle. 92pp.
36. (Vol. 6 No. 4) **Faith and the World of Politics.** Ed. Johannes Baptist Metz. 96pp.
37. (Vol. 7 No. 4) **Prophecy.** Ed. Roger Aubert. 80pp.
38. (Vol. 8 No. 4) **Order and the Sacraments.** Ed. Neophytos Edelby and Teodoro Jimenez Urresti. 96pp.
39. (Vol. 9 No. 4) **Christian Life and Eschatology.** Ed. Christian Duquoc. 94pp.
40. (Vol. 10 No. 4) **The Eucharist: Celebrating the Presence of the Lord.** Ed. Pierre Benoit and Roland Murphy. 88pp.
41. (Vol. 1 No. 5) **Dogma.** Ed. Edward Schillebeeckx. 84pp.
42. (Vol. 2 No. 5) **The Future of the Liturgy.** Ed. Johannes Wagner. 92pp.
43. (Vol. 3 No. 5) **The Ministry and Life of Priests Today.** Ed. Karl Rahner. 104pp.
44. (Vol. 4 No. 5) **Courage Needed.** Ed. Hans Küng. 92pp.
45. (Vol. 5 No. 5) **Profession and Responsibility in Society.** Ed. Franz Bockle. 84pp.
46. (Vol. 6 No. 5) **Fundamental Theology.** Ed. Johannes Baptist Metz. 84pp.
47. (Vol. 7 No. 5) **Sacralization in the History of the Church.** Ed. Roger Aubert. 80pp.
48. (Vol. 8 No. 5) **The Dynamism of Canon Law.** Ed. Neophytos Edelby and Teodoro Jimenez Urresti. 92pp.
49. (Vol. 9 No. 5) **An Anxious Society Looks to the Gospel.** Ed. Christian Duquoc. 80pp.
50. (Vol. 10 No. 5) **The Presence and Absence of God.** Ed. Pierre Benoit and Roland Murphy. 88pp.
51. (Vol. 1 No. 6) **Tension between Church and Faith.** Ed. Edward Schillebeeckx. 160pp.
52. (Vol. 2 No. 6) **Prayer and Community.** Ed. Herman Schmidt. 156pp.
53. (Vol. 3 No. 6) **Catechetics for the Future.** Ed. Alois Müller. 168pp.
54. (Vol. 4 No. 6) **Post-Ecumenical Christianity.** Ed. Hans Küng. 168pp.
55. (Vol. 5 No. 6) **The Future of Marriage as Institution.** Ed. Franz Bockle. 180pp.
56. (Vol. 6 No. 6) **Moral Evil Under Challenge.** Ed. Johannes Baptist Metz. 160pp.
57. (Vol. 7 No. 6) **Church History at a Turning Point.** Ed. Roger Aubert. 160pp.
58. (Vol. 8 No. 6) **Structures of the Church's Presence in the World of Today.** Ed. Teodoro Jimenez Urresti. 160pp.
59. (Vol. 9 No. 6) **Hope.** Ed. Christian Duquoc. 160pp.
60. (Vol. 10 No. 6) **Immortality and Resurrection.** Ed. Pierre Benoit and Roland Murphy. 160pp.
61. (Vol. 1 No. 7) **The Sacramental Administration of Reconciliation.** Ed. Edward Schillebeeckx. 160pp
62. (Vol. 2 No. 7) **Worship of Christian Man Today.** Ed. Herman Schmidt. 156pp.
63. (Vol. 3 No. 7) **Democratization of the Church.** Ed. Alois Müller. 160pp.
64. (Vol. 4 No. 7) **The Petrine Ministry in the Church.** Ed. Hans Küng. 160pp.
65. (Vol. 5 No. 7) **The Manipulation of Man.** Ed. Franz Bockle. 144pp
66. (Vol. 6 No. 7) **Fundamental Theology in the Church.** Ed. Johannes Baptist Metz. 156pp.
67. (Vol. 7 No. 7) **The Self-Understanding of the Church.** Ed. Roger Aubert. 144pp.
68. (Vol. 8 No. 7) **Contestation in the Church.** Ed. Teodoro Jimenez Urresti. 152pp.
69. (Vol. 9 No. 7) **Spirituality, Public or Private?** Ed. Christian Duquoc. 156pp.
70. (Vol. 10 No. 7) **Theology, Exegesis and Proclamation.** Ed. Roland Murphy. 144pp.
71. (Vol. 1 No. 8) **The Bishop and the Unity of the Church.** Ed. Edward Schillebeeckx. 156pp.
72. (Vol. 2 No. 8) **Liturgy and the Ministry.** Ed. Herman Schmidt. 160pp.
73. (Vol. 3 No. 8) **Reform of the Church.** Ed. Alois Müller and Norbert Greinacher. 152pp.
74. (Vol. 4 No. 8) **Mutual Recognition of Ecclesial Ministries?** Ed. Hans Küng and Walter Kasper. 152pp
75. (Vol. 5 No. 8) **Man in a New Society.** Ed. Franz Bockle. 160pp
76. (Vol. 6 No. 8) **The God Question.** Ed. Johannes Baptist Metz. 156pp.
77. (Vol. 7 No. 8) **Election-Consensus-Reception.** Ed. Giuseppe Alberigo and Anton Weiler. 156pp.
78. (Vol. 8 No. 8) **Celibacy of the Catholic Priest.** Ed. William Bassett and Peter Huizing. 160pp
79. (Vol. 9 No. 8) **Prayer.** Ed. Christian Duquoc and Claude Geffré. 126pp.
80. (Vol. 10 No. 8) **Ministries in the Church.** Ed. Bas van Iersel and Roland Murphy. 152pp.
81. **The Persistence of Religion.** Andrew Greeley and Gregory Baum. 0 8164 2537 X 168pp.
82. **Liturgical Experience of Faith.** Herman Schmidt and David Power. 0 8164 2538 8 144pp.
83. **Truth and Certainty.** Ed. Edward Schillebeeckx and Bas van Iersel. 0 8164 2539 6 144pp.
84. **Political Commitment and Christian Community.** Ed. Alois Müller and Norbert Greinacher. 0 8164 2540 X 156pp.
85. **The Crisis of Religious Language.** Ed. Johannes Baptist Metz and Jean-Pierre Jossua. 0 8164 2541 144pp.
86. **Humanism and Christianity.** Ed. Claude Geffré. 0 8164 2542 6 144pp.
87. **The Future of Christian Marriage.** Ed. William Bassett and Peter Huizing. 0 8164 2575 2.

88. **Polarization in the Church.** Ed. Hans Küng and Walter Kasper. 0 8164 2572 8 156pp.

89. **Spiritual Revivals.** Ed. Christian Duquoc and Casiano Floristán. 0 8164 2573 6 156pp.

90. **Power and the Word of God.** Ed. Franz Bockle and Jacques Marie Pohier. 0 8164 2574 4 156pp.

91. **The Church as Institution.** Ed. Gregory Baum and Andrew Greeley. 0 8164 2575 2 168pp.

92. **Politics and Liturgy.** Ed. Herman Schmidt and David Power. 0 8164 2576 0 156pp.

93. **Jesus Christ and Human Freedom.** Ed. Edward Schillebeeckx and Bas van Iersel. 0 8164 2577 9 168pp.

4. **The Experience of Dying.** Ed. Norbert Greinacher and Alois Müller. 0 8164 2578 7 156pp.

5. **Theology of Joy.** Ed. Johannes Baptist Metz and Jean-Pierre Jossua. 0 8164 2579 5 164pp.

6. **The Mystical and Political Dimension of the Christian Faith.** Ed. Claude Geffré and Gustavo Guttierez. 0 8164 2580 9 168pp.

7. **The Future of the Religious Life.** Ed. Peter Huizing and William Bassett. 0 8164 2094 7 96pp.

8. **Christians and Jews.** Ed. Hans Küng and Walter Kasper. 0 8164 2095 5 96pp.

9. **Experience of the Spirit.** Ed. Peter Huizing and William Bassett. 0 8164 2096 3 144pp.

10. **Sexuality in Contemporary Catholicism.** Ed. Franz Bockle and Jacques Marie Pohier. 0 8164 2097 1 126pp.

11. **Ethnicity.** Ed. Andrew Greeley and Gregory Baum. 0 8164 2145 5 120pp.

12. **Liturgy and Cultural Religious Traditions.** Ed. Herman Schmidt and David Power. 0 8164 2146 2 120pp.

13. **A Personal God?** Ed. Edward Schillebeeckx and Bas van Iersel. 0 8164 2149 8 142pp.

14. **The Poor and the Church.** Ed. Norbert Greinacher and Alois Müller. 0 8164 2147 1 128pp.

15. **Christianity and Socialism.** Ed. Johannes Baptist Metz and Jean-Pierre Jossua. 0 8164 2148 X 144pp.

16. **The Churches of Africa: Future Prospects.** Ed. Claude Geffré and Bertrand Luneau. 0 8164 2150 1 128pp.

17. **Judgement in the Church.** Ed. William Bassett and Peter Huizing. 0 8164 2166 8 128pp.

18. **Why Did God Make Me?** Ed. Hans Küng and Jürgen Moltmann. 0 8164 2167 6 112pp.

19. **Charisms in the Church.** Ed. Christian Duquoc and Casiano Floristán. 0 8164 2168 4 128pp.

20. **Moral Formation and Christianity.** Ed. Franz Bockle and Jacques Marie Pohier. 0 8164 2169 2 120pp.

Communication in the Church. Ed. Gregory Baum and Andrew Greeley. 0 8164 2170 6 126pp.

112. **Liturgy and Human Passage.** Ed. David Power and Luis Maldonado. 0 8164 2608 2 136pp.

113. **Revelation and Experience.** Ed. Edward Schillebeeckx and Bas van Iersel. 0 8164 2609 0 134pp.

114. **Evangelization in the World Today.** Ed. Norbert Greinacher and Alois Müller. 0 8164 2610 4 136pp.

115. **Doing Theology in New Places.** Ed. Jean-Pierre Jossua and Johannes Baptist Metz. 0 8164 2611 2 120pp.

116. **Buddhism and Christianity.** Ed. Claude Geffré and Mariasusai Dhavamony. 0 8164 2612 0 136pp.

117. **The Finances of the Church.** Ed. William Bassett and Peter Huizing. 0 8164 2197 8 160pp.

118. **An Ecumenical Confession of Faith?** Ed. Hans Küng and Jürgen Moltmann. 0 8164 2198 6 136pp.

119. **Discernment of the Spirit and of Spirits.** Ed. Casiano Floristán and Christian Duquoc. 0 8164 2199 4 136pp.

120. **The Death Penalty and Torture.** Ed. Franz Bockle and Jacques Marie Pohier. 0 8164 2200 1 136pp.

121. **The Family in Crisis or in Transition.** Ed. Andrew Greeley. 0 567 30001 3 128pp.

122. **Structures of Initiation in Crisis.** Ed. Luis Maldonado and David Power. 0 567 30002 1 128pp.

123. **Heaven.** Ed. Bas van Iersel and Edward Schillebeeckx. 0 567 30003 X 120pp.

124. **The Church and the Rights of Man.** Ed. Alois Müller and Norbert Greinacher. 0 567 30004 8 140pp.

125. **Christianity and the Bourgeoisie.** Ed. Johannes Baptist Metz. 0 567 30005 6 144pp.

126. **China as a Challenge to the Church.** Ed. Claude Geffré and Joseph Spae. 0 567 30006 4 136pp.

127. **The Roman Curia and the Communion of Churches.** Ed. Peter Huizing and Knut Walf. 0 567 30007 2 144pp.

128. **Conflicts about the Holy Spirit.** Ed. Hans Küng and Jürgen Moltmann. 0 567 30008 0 144pp.

129. **Models of Holiness.** Ed. Christian Duquoc and Casiano Floristán. 0 567 30009 9 128pp.

130. **The Dignity of the Despised of the Earth.** Ed. Jacques Marie Pohier and Dietmar Mieth. 0 567 30010 2 144pp.

131. **Work and Religion.** Ed. Gregory Baum. 0 567 30011 0 148pp.

132. **Symbol and Art in Worship.** Ed. Luis Maldonado and David Power. 0 567 30012 9 136pp.

133. **Right of the Community to a Priest.** Ed. Edward Schillebeeckx and Johannes Baptist Metz. 0 567 30013 7 148pp.

134. **Women in a Men's Church.** Ed. Virgil Elizondo and Norbert Greinacher. 0 567 30014 5 144pp.

135. **True and False Universality of Christianity.** Ed. Claude Geffré and Jean-Pierre Jossua. 0 567 30015 3 138pp.

136. **What is Religion? An Inquiry for Christian Theology.** Ed. Mircea Eliade and David Tracy. 0 567 30016 1 98pp.

137. **Electing our Own Bishops.** Ed. Peter Huizing and Knut Walf. 0 567 30017 X 112pp.

138. **Conflicting Ways of Interpreting the Bible.** Ed. Hans Küng and Jürgen Moltmann. 0 567 30018 8 112pp.

139. **Christian Obedience.** Ed. Casiano Floristán and Christian Duquoc. 0 567 30019 6 96pp.

140. **Christian Ethics and Economics: the North-South Conflict.** Ed. Dietmar Mieth and Jacques Marie Pohier. 0 567 30020 X 128pp.

141. **Neo-Conservatism: Social and Religious Phenomenon.** Ed. Gregory Baum and John Coleman. 0 567 30021 8.

142. **The Times of Celebration.** Ed. David Power and Mary Collins. 0 567 30022 6.

143. **God as Father.** Ed. Edward Schillebeeckx and Johannes Baptist Metz. 0 567 30023 4.

144. **Tensions Between the Churches of the First World and the Third World.** Ed. Virgil Elizondo and Norbert Greinacher. 0 567 30024 2.

145. **Nietzsche and Christianity.** Ed. Claude Geffré and Jean-Pierre Jossua. 0 567 30025 0.

146. **Where Does the Church Stand?** Ed. Giuseppe Alberigo. 0 567 30026 9.

147. **The Revised Code of Canon Law: a Missed Opportunity?** Ed. Peter Huizing and Knut Walf. 0 567 30027 7.

148. **Who Has the Say in the Church?** Ed. Hans Küng and Jürgen Moltmann. 0 567 30028 5.

149. **Francis of Assisi Today.** Ed. Casiano Floristán and Christian Duquoc. 0 567 30029 3.

150. **Christian Ethics: Uniformity, Universality, Pluralism.** Ed. Jacques Pohier and Dietmar Mieth. 0 567 30030 7.

151. **The Church and Racism.** Ed. Gregory Baum and John Coleman. 0 567 30031 5.

152. **Can we always celebrate the Eucharist?** Ed. Mary Collins and David Power. 0 567 30032 3.

153. **Jesus, Son of God?** Ed. Edward Schillebeeckx and Johannes-Baptist Metz. 0 567 30033 1.

154. **Religion and Churches in Eastern Europe.** Ed. Virgil ELizondo and Norbert Greinacher. 0 567 30034 X.

155. **'The Human', Criterion of Christian Existence?** Ed. Claude Geffré and Jean-Pierre Jossua. 0 567 30035 8.

156. **The Challenge of Psychology to Faith.** Ed. Steven Kepnes (Guest Editor) and David Tracy. 0 567 30036 6.

157. **May Church Ministers be Politicians?** Ed. Peter Huizing and Knut Walf. 0 567 30037 4.

158. **The Right to Dissent.** Ed. Hans Küng and Jürgen Moltmann. 0 567 30038 2.

CONCILIUM

159. **Learning to pray.** Ed. Casiano Floristán and Christian Duquoc. 0 567 30039 0.
160. **Unemployment and the Right to Work.** Ed. Dietmar Mieth and Jacques Pohier. 0 567 30040 4.
161. **New Religious Movements.** Ed. by John Coleman and Gregory Baum.
162. **Liturgy: A Creative Tradition.** Ed. by Mary Collins and David Power.
163. **Martyrdom Today.** Ed. by Johannes-Baptist Metz and Edward Schillebeeckx.
164. **Church and Peace.** Ed. by Virgil Elizondo and Norbert Greinacher.
165. **Indifference to Religion.** Ed. by Claude Geffré and Jean-Pierre Jossua.
166. **Theology and Cosmology.** Ed. by David Tracy and Nicholas Lash.
167. **The Ecumenical Council and the Church Constitution.** Ed. by Peter Huizing and Knut Walf.
168. **Mary in the Churches.** Ed. by Hans Küng and Jürgen Moltmann.
169. **Job and the Silence of God.** Ed. by Christian Duquoc and Casiano Floristán.

170. **Twenty Years of Concilium—Retrospect and Prospect.** Ed. by Edward Schillebeeckx, Paul Brand and Anton Weiler.
171. **Different Theologies, Common Responsibility: Babel or Pentecost?** Ed. by C. Geffre, G. Gutierrez, V. Elizondo.
172. **The Ethics of Liberation—The Liberation of Ethics.** Ed. by D. Mieth, J. Pohier.
173. **The Sexual Revolution.** Ed. by G. Baum, J. Coleman.
174. **The Transmission of the Faith to the Next Generation.** Ed. by V. Elizondo, D. Tracy.
175. **The Holocaust as Interruption.** Ed. by E. Fiorenza, D. Tracy.
176. **La Iglesia Popular: Between Fear and Hope.** Ed. by L. Boff, V. Elizondo.
177. **Monotheism.** Ed. by Claude Geffré and Jean Pierre Jossua.
178. **Blessing and Power.** Ed. by David Power and Mary Collins.

179. **Suicide and the Right to Die.** Ed. by Jacques Pohier and Dietmar Mieth.
180. **The Teaching Authority of the Believers.** Ed. by Johannes-Baptist Metz and Edward Schillibeeckx.
181. **Youth Without a Future?** Ed. by John Coleman and Gregory Baum.
182. **Women—Invisible in Church and Theology.** Ed. by Elisabeth Fiorenza and Mary Collins.
183. **Christianity Among World Religions.** Ed. by Hans Küng and Jürgen Moltmann.
184. **Forgiveness.** Ed. by Casiano Floristán and Christian Duquoc.
185. **Canon Law—Church Reality.** Ed. by James Provost and Knut Walf.
186. **Popular Religion.** Ed. by Norbert Greinacher and Norbert Mette.
187. **Option for the Poor! Challenge to the Rich Countries.** Ed. by Leonardo Boff and Virgil Elizondo.
188. **Synod 1985: An Evaluation.** Ed. by Giuseppe Alberigo and James Provost.

CONCILIUM 1987

THE EXODUS
Edited by Bas van Iersel and Anton Weiler   189

THE FATE OF CONFESSION
Edited by Mary Collins and David Power   190

CHANGING VALUES AND VIRTUES
Edited by Dietmar Mieth and
Jacques Pohier   191

ORTHODOXY AND HETERODOXY
Edited by Johannes-Baptist Metz
and Edward Schillebeeckx   192

THE CHURCH AND CHRISTIAN DEMOCRACY
Edited by Gregory Baum and John Coleman   193

WOMEN, WORK AND POVERTY
Edited by Elisabeth Schüssler Fiorenza
and Anne Carr   194

All back issues are still in print: available from bookshops (price £5.45) or direct from the publishers (£5.95/US$9.95/Can$11.75 including postage and packing).

T & T CLARK LTD, 59 GEORGE STREET EDINBURGH EH2 2LQ, SCOTLAND

Fifty Years of Catholic Theology

Yves Congar edited by
Bernard Lauret

Conversations with Yves Congar on change in the Catholic church
£4.95   *paper*

Theology from the Womb of Asia

Choan-Seng Song

Faith explored in the midst of Asian culture to establish an indigenous theology
£8.95   *paper*

God, Politics and the Future

David E Jenkins

The Bishop of Durham talks about industry, big business, poverty, the inner city, ecology, peace, and the churches' role in our divided society.
£4.95   *paper*

Jesus: The Unanswered Questions

John Bowden

Can we in fact know anything about Jesus?
£9.50   *paper*

Above the Treeline

Towards a Contemporary Spirituality

Heije Faber

A deeper view of life is developed on the model of an expedition into the hills, from the valley to the summit far ahead, above the treeline. Faber provides encouragement and stimulus for all those in search of a viable contemporary spirituality.
paper   £5.95

Christianity and the Goddesses

Susanne Heine

Warns against the revival of the cult of the goddesses and the earth mother in feminist theology.
£6.95   *paper*

SCM PRESS LTD

26–30 Tottenham Road
London N1 4BZ